Digital Selling

How to use social media and the web to generate leads and sell more

Grant Leboff

Kogan Page

LONDON PHILADELPHIA NEW DELHI

First published in Great Britain and the United States in 2016 by Kogan Page Limited

2nd Floor, 45 Gee Street	1518 Walnut Street,	4737/23 Ansari Road
London	Suite 900	Daryaganj
EC1V 3RS	Philadelphia PA 19102	New Delhi 110002
United Kingdom	USA	India

www.koganpage.com

© Grant Leboff, 2016

The right of Grant Leboff to be identified as the author of this work has been asserted by him in accordance with the Copyright, Designs and Patents Act 1988.

ISBN   978 0 7494 7507 9
E-ISBN   978 0 7494 7508 6

British Library Cataloguing-in-Publication Data

A CIP record for this book is available from the British Library.

Library of Congress Cataloging-in-Publication Data
Names: Leboff, Grant, author.
Title: Digital selling : how to use social media and the web to generate
   leads and sell more / Grant Leboff.
Description: 1st Edition. | Philadelphia, PA : Kogan Page, 2016. | Includes
   bibliographical references and index.
Identifiers: LCCN 2016025650 (print) | LCCN 2016034217 (ebook) | ISBN
   9780749475079 (paperback) | ISBN 9780749475086 (ebook)
Subjects: LCSH: Telemarketing. | Electronic commerce. | Selling. | BISAC:
   BUSINESS & ECONOMICS / Sales & Selling. | BUSINESS & ECONOMICS / Marketing
   / General. | BUSINESS & ECONOMICS / E-Commerce / Internet Marketing. |
   BUSINESS & ECONOMICS / Advertising & Promotion.
Classification: LCC HF5415.1265 .L426 2016 (print) | LCC HF5415.1265 (ebook)
   | DDC 658.8/72–dc23
LC record available at https://lccn.loc.gov/2016025650

Typeset by SPi Global
Print production managed by Jellyfish
Printed and bound by CPI Group (UK) Ltd, Croydon, CR0 4YY

PRAISE FOR
DIGITAL SELLING

'In this terrific book Grant Leboff provides readers with a sales model for the digital age. This is a vital read for all those involved in any growing organization.' **Zev Siegl, Keynote Presenter, Co-founder, Starbucks Coffee Company**

'A powerful and timely explanation of how the role and activities of salespeople must fundamentally change in this digital era.' **Jay Baer, President, Convince & Convert, and author of *Hug Your Haters***

'*Digital Selling* not only challenges existing thinking about the most efficacious sales processes for today but also presents practical solutions based on experience to allow companies to start to generate greater success in this fast-moving area.' **Andrew Peters, Managing Director, Siemens Digital Factory, UK**

'Grant Leboff's *Sticky Marketing* was a game changer for us in how we approached our marketing strategy. Now his new book, *Digital Selling*, has got the potential to deliver the very same impact for our sales teams across Europe. The book offers valuable insights into the new digital era, draws from real-world examples and provides practical advice for the business. A must-read!' **Helen Whitten, Head of European Marketing Communications, Roland Europe Group Limited**

'*Digital Selling* meets the challenges of the modern salesperson head on and provides many of the answers. It is a book I found not just thought-provoking, but also provided real insight and understanding. It is a must-read and I highly recommend it.' **Jack Mizel, CEO, Institute of Sales Management**

'Customers are changing the way they purchase and in this excellent book Grant Leboff explains how businesses can get in front of more prospects and turn them into customers by using social media and the web effectively.' **Jonathan Quin, CEO, World First**

'If you want to learn how to use social media and the web to sell more you must read Grant Leboff's new book, *Digital Selling*. The book brilliantly explains how customers have changed the way they buy and how we all need to change the way we market and sell.' **Jon Ferrara, CEO, Nimble**

'This book makes sense of so many of the challenges facing salespeople today. It is packed with great advice on how salespeople can use the web and social media effectively. A great book from one of today's thought leaders on sales and marketing.' **Ben Turner, Managing Director, Association of Professional Sales**

'At last, a book that not only confirms what sales in a digital world should be, but one that outlines WHY and HOW. This is a MUST-READ for any Sales Director and for anyone who's serious about professional selling in a digital world.' **Steve Gilroy, Chief Executive, Vistage International (UK) Ltd**

'Grant Leboff has greater awareness than many in the sales and marketing game of how the sales process has changed in the past few years. Learn from him how better to focus on the right and profitable wins, the clever investment focus for your marketing and sales planning to maximize sales opportunities and growth.' **Lara Morgan, Investor in GB invention**

'*Digital Selling* is another belter of a book from Grant Leboff. He explains brilliantly the context of selling in a digital world. As always he combines practical insight with rich anecdote. A thoroughly enjoyable, informative and essential read for anyone looking to scale their business!' **Duncan Cheatle, Founder, Rise To, Prelude Group and Co-founder, StartUp Britain**

'*Digital Selling* will prove to be a valuable read for any business leader, marketing or sales professional... which I can highly recommend.' **Ian Price, Chief Executive, Academy for Chief Executives**

'*Digital Selling* brilliantly explains the opportunities that social media and the web provide today's salespeople with. A must-read from one of the UK's leading sales and marketers.' **Conor Morris, Executive Chairman, The Sales Institute of Ireland**

CONTENTS

LIST OF ABBREVIATIONS

ADSL: Asymmetric Digital Subscriber Line

AIDA: Awareness, Interest, Desire, Action

AM: Ante Meridiem (before midday)

App: Application

ARPANET: The Advanced Research Projects Agency Network

B2B: Business to Business

B2C: Business to Consumer

BBC: British Broadcasting Corporation

CEI: Competitive Enterprise Institute

CEO: Chief Executive Officer

CERN: Conseil Européen pour la Recherche Nucléaire (European Council for Nuclear Research)

CIO: Chief Information Officer

CNN: Cable News Network

COO: Chief Operations Officer

CRM: Customer relationship management

CV: Curriculum vitae (Latin for 'course of life')

ET: Eastern Time

FAQ: Frequently Asked Questions

FTC: Federal Trade Commission

GIF: The Graphics Interchange Format

HP: Hewlett-Packard

HR: Human Resources

IBM: International Business Machines

iOS: Apple Inc., operating system

IP: Internet Protocol

IT:	Information Technology
ITV:	Independent Television News
KPI:	Key Performance Indicator
Ofcom:	The communications regulator in the United Kingdom
Plc:	Public Limited Company
PM:	Post Meridiem (after midday)
R&D:	Research and Development
ROI:	Return on Investment
SMS:	Short Message Service
TV:	Television
UCLA:	The University of California, Los Angeles
UK:	United Kingdom
USA:	United States of America
USP:	Unique Selling Point or Unique Selling Proposition
VHF:	Very High Frequency
WiFi:	A facility allowing computers, smartphones, or other devices to connect to the internet or communicate with one another wirelessly within a particular area

Prologue

Are you suffering from Pike Syndrome?

In 1873 a German zoologist, Dr. Karl Möbius,[1] conducted a famous experiment, the result of which has come to be known as 'Pike Syndrome'.[2] Since then the experiment has been repeated innumerable times.

A pike, which is a predatory fish, is put in a tank with a number of minnows. The minnows are separated from the pike by a clear glass divider or bottle. The pike can see the minnows but every time it goes to eat them it smashes its face into the glass.

After several hours, the pike gives up trying to eat the minnows. At this point the glass divider is removed, and the pike is free to eat the minnows whenever it wants. However, the pike makes no attempt to eat the minnows. Having previously found them unattainable, it will never again try to eat the minnows, even when they are swimming freely through the tank merely a few millimetres away from the pike.

In the original experiment, Dr. Möbius subsequently fed the pike himself, but others have allowed the pike to die of starvation, which it will do despite the fact that food is freely available.

It is hard to understand how a pike could die, rather than make any more attempts to try to eat the food that would keep it alive. To many it is unfathomable that the pike can't comprehend the paradigm shift that takes place when the minnows are released and disseminate freely throughout the tank.

Yet, this is happening in sales all the time. We are living through an era of profound change. Despite the developments in communications and buyer behaviour, many individuals fail to alter their own practices and react to the fundamental transformations that have taken place.

Why, when selling, do people:

- Still insist on giving pedestrian presentations when prospects can, and often do, obtain all the standard information from the web?

- Persist with 'cold calling' as a major lead-generating activity which, in an era of customers having unprecedented levels of information and choice, is becoming increasingly ineffective?[3]

- Remain reliant on a traditional sales funnel,[4] first developed in 1898 and consequently not the best model almost 120 years later when communications have fundamentally changed?

Too many organizations are using outdated sales models, relying on obsolete systems and methods from a bygone era.

The paradigm has been altered. The minnows are swimming freely through the tank. The glass bowl has been lifted.

If you are looking for a new product or service today, your starting point will probably be the same two places:

1 You will ask your networks of family, friends, colleagues and business associates.

2 You will go online and search.

Now, even these two channels are converging.

The 'referral' has always been the ultimate prize for any salesperson. Having been recommended by a friend or colleague, the prospect is often predisposed to buy. Therefore, word-of-mouth recommendations have always been the most effective route to market for anybody trying to sell anything.

This is because social proof is one of the biggest influencers on human behaviour; that is, what others say and do. This is why we ask our networks for guidance and observe the purchasing decisions that people around us make. It feels safe. Recommendations from friends and colleagues take a lot of the perceived risk out of any acquisition.

One of the biggest changes the web, social media and digital technology have engendered is that we now live in a world where everyone has a channel. People can voice their opinions about anything and have a much wider influence than they could possibly have imagined before the digital era.

This does not make every individual a broadcaster in the sense of CNN, Fox or the BBC, although social platforms have produced a plethora of internet stars. It does, however, make many individuals 'narrowcasters'. That is, amongst their family, friends, peers, colleagues and industry they can have an influence way beyond anything previously achieved.

We live in a world where information is increasingly distributed through social networks via conversation, rather than publication.[5] The result is that two of the most likely places any prospect will look for a supplier, via a web search or from a word-of-mouth recommendation, are becoming one and the same.

As social media becomes ubiquitous and continues to influence search results, and as the web results in people being increasingly connected, social proof matters more. This is not because it has become more powerful – it was always one of the most important influencers on human behaviour – rather, it is because it is now more accessible in an increasing number of the decisions we make.

In this environment, why are those individuals who need to sell their products and services not:

- Utilizing these digital channels to communicate and influence buyers in the places they are really looking?

- Building their own reputation amongst the relevant communities so they become known, and therefore a 'go to' person within their field of expertise?

- Re-evaluating the sales model to create something more appropriate for selling in the 21st century?

Digital selling is an answer to these questions. Digital selling:

- presents a new funnel, more appropriate and aligned with effective selling in a digital era;

- provides a mindset which must be adopted to meet today's sales challenges;

- focuses on the activities to be undertaken in order to achieve success.

Ultimately, digital selling is about leveraging the power of digital media, to prospect and nurture leads in an effective way in order to create sales opportunities.

Just as the postal service, telephone and e-mail transformed the way we communicate in the workplace, social media is doing the same. 'Social Business' means social channels will be increasingly used, both internally and externally, to interact with suppliers, colleagues and customers.

While the challenge for business will be channelling these efforts to create a cohesive and focused organization able to deliver effectively for its customers, the opportunities are tremendous. It has never been quicker or easier to exchange ideas, make suggestions and, therefore, collaborate with suppliers, colleagues and customers.

In this business environment, it is essential that those involved with selling utilize these digital tools effectively. Digital selling will show you how to use social media and the web to generate leads and sell more.

Endnotes

1 Dr. Karl August Möbius: The Editors of Encyclopædia Britannica (undated) Karl August Möbius. *Encyclopedia Britannica* [online] http://www.britannica.com/biography/Karl-August-Mobius [accessed 9 October 2015]

'Karl August Möbius (born Feb. 7, 1825, Eilenburg, Prussia [Germany] – died April 26, 1908, Ger.) German zoologist who is chiefly known for his contributions to marine biology.'

2 I want to thank Daniel Schreiber for introducing me to the Pike Syndrome experiment.

3 Cold Calling: Barbara Giamanco and Kent Gregoire (2012) Tweet me, friend me, make me buy, *Harvard Business Review*, July–August [online] https://hbr.org/2012/07/tweet-me-friend-me-make-me-buy [accessed 9 October 2015]

'... the return on cold calling is dropping with every passing year. Indeed, in a recent survey by InsideView, an online provider of sales-relevant content, more than 90% of C-level executives said they 'never' respond to cold calls or e-mail blasts.'

4 Purchase Funnel: Scott Anderson Miller (undated) What is Lewis's Purchase Funnel? *Inbound Marketing For Dummies* [online] http://www.dummies.com/how-to/content/what-is-lewiss-purchase-funnel.html [accessed 24 Dec 2015]

'In 1898, Elias St. Elmo Lewis developed what was called the Purchase Funnel. It was based on the idea that for a sale to occur, every consumer must take the same steps toward a purchase.'

5 Information distribution: American Press Institute (2014) Social and demographic differences in news habits and attitudes, *America Press Institute*, 17 March [online] http://www.americanpressinstitute.org/publications/reports/survey-research/social-demographic-differences-news-habits-attitudes/ [accessed 9 October 2015]

The report leads with the findings that 71 per cent of younger adults (18–29) are more likely to find news through social media than adults over 60 (21 per cent). The report continues: *'A majority of 30–39-year-olds also discover news through social media (64 per cent), as do 41 per cent of 40–59-year-olds. Similarly, people under 40 are more likely than those 40 and over to discover news through internet searches and online news aggregators.'*

Why embracing the social web is vital   01

We no longer require a publishing company to get our words read or a record company to have our music heard. We can distribute video without the need for a media organization and can have our opinions listened to, beyond our small network of friends and family, without them being carried by newspapers, radio or television.

Quite simply, we are living in the social era. This concept, however, is often misinterpreted. It does not mean that for the first time in history human beings are talking to each other! Nor does it imply that we are any more, or less, social than in previous generations, though there are many individuals who would try to argue this one way or the other.

Instead, it refers to a phenomenon that quite simply changes many of the paradigms to which we traditionally adhered. The transformation is stark. The consequences are enormous. The fundamental development is simply this:

For the first time in history everyone has a channel.

This phenomenon changes so many traditional principles by which we have previously lived. In order to get some perspective, however, it is useful to put into context how we arrived at this juncture.

Built in 1943, Colossus was the world's first electronic digital programmable computer.[1] Used by the allies to read encrypted messages being sent from the German high command to their army, it led to the development of commercial computers in the 1950s.

In the 1960s, the idea of computers connected across the globe, to enable the sharing of data and programs, started to be discussed.

In 1969, the first host-to-host message was sent via the ARPANET.[2] The internet[3] grew out of ARPANET and by the mid-1980s the internet was well established.

At the end of 1990, Sir Tim Berners-Lee served the first web page on the open internet.[4] The significance of the world wide web is that it allowed information to be shared extensively with ease. Up until then, in order to access material on the internet, individuals would have to log on to different computers, often using a variety of programs. With the agreement, in 1993, that the underlying code of the world wide web would be available royalty free to everyone forever, the web really took off.[5]

However, the slow speed at which people could dial into the web hampered how useful it was. Often, it was quicker to go and look something up in a book than try to conduct a web search. This all changed in the first few years of the 21st century, as broadband started to become widely available.[6]

Although the first social media site, as we would understand it today, was Six Degrees, launched in 1997,[7] it is no coincidence that social media did not really take hold until the early 2000s.[8] After all, with slow dial-up speeds, it was easier for most people to call friends than to try to communicate online.

Wider access to broadband started to make social media useful. In fact, the oldest social media sites, still widely in use today, are LinkedIn, which was launched on 5 May 2003,[9] and Facebook, which began on 4 February 2004.[10] It is no coincidence, perhaps, that both of these sites became successful in an age of wider broadband availability.

Finally, smartphones began to become popular, culminating with the launch of the first iPhone in 2007.[11] As an increasing number of people purchased these devices, social media exploded. Once social networks could be accessed anytime and anywhere, the value they provided in being able to share moments and stay in contact with friends 24/7, meant that, for an ever-increasing number of individuals, they became the communication channel of choice. It is this combination of social media platforms and the smartphone that means today, everyone can own their own media channels and can share moments, opinions and thoughts with the rest of the world.

These technological advances have seen a shift in scarcity and abundance. We used to inhabit a world where access to knowledge, in relative terms, was scarce. There were not that many places one could go to obtain information on available products or services. Yellow Pages or Business Pages may indicate some possible suppliers, trade magazines or consumer titles might provide some market knowledge and, of course, one could visit libraries to undertake further research. However, it was all quite limited in scope.

A consequence of this situation was that we were also restricted in choice. It was often hard enough trying to identify and interact with appropriate vendors locally, let alone attempting to go further afield, so we were normally stuck using the suppliers that were nearby.

In a world where access to information and choice were, in relative terms, scarce, what was abundant was attention. We had fewer distractions than we have today. There was not the myriad of e-mails, texts, messaging services, apps, social networks and digital TV and radio channels, all continually accessible, thanks to the smartphone. Therefore, if we were in the market for a particular product or service, we were often predisposed to giving consideration to any opportunities or communications that came our way.

In this environment, prospects and customers were often very willing to meet with salespeople. For example, a CEO of a small business looking to recruit new staff might decide to use a recruitment company to assist them. However, the CEO would know nothing of the market, current costs, terms and conditions and what to expect.

Of course, the CEO may have asked some colleagues; after all, we have always utilized word of mouth. They may have looked through Yellow Pages or Business Pages in order to identify some potential providers of the service, but then what? Before the age of the web, the easiest recourse was often to have a few meetings with possible suppliers. After two or three encounters with promising companies, the CEO would have a reasonable idea of what to expect and could start to make some decisions.

In this previous era, salespeople provided value merely by turning up. A salesperson visiting a prospect's office and explaining how they worked could provide the prospect with knowledge that they had no other way of obtaining. Therefore, at the appropriate time, it was usual for salespeople to be able to get some 'face time' with prospects and customers.

The creation of the world wide web and social media has completely altered this situation. Information is now abundant. In most areas of our lives, we no longer struggle to access material. In fact, our challenge is often information overload. There is now often so much that sorting out the wheat from the chaff is normally a bigger task than finding the knowledge in the first place.

In a world where everyone has a channel, there is now a copious amount of material available. Before the world wide web, it was mainly publishing and media companies that produced communications for wider consumption, through books, newspapers, magazines, television programmes, films and music, etc. Of course, these companies are still producing content. In fact, today most are producing more material, as digital has increased the number of channels they are trying to fill.

For example, from the years 1964–1990, in the UK, the British Broadcasting Corporation (BBC) had two television channels, four national radio stations and a local radio presence throughout the country.[12] Amongst its offering now are 10 national TV channels, 10 national radio stations plus local radio throughout the UK, and an extensive online offering via its website.[13] Digital has forced many other media companies to grow in the same way.

Meanwhile, businesses themselves have become media entities. In owning websites, blogs, YouTube channels, LinkedIn pages, Facebook pages, Google+ pages, Twitter, Pinterest and Instagram accounts, etc., organizations have also become media companies. These channels are only as good as the content that is put on them, and so companies are putting out material in ways they never did previously.

Finally, every individual is now potentially a mini media company. Just as organizations have channels they have to fill with content, individuals are also utilizing social platforms and sharing thoughts and information. The culmination of all of this is that information is not just abundant, it is prolific.

This easy access to vast amounts of knowledge, together with technological advancement, means choice is now also abundant. The barriers to market, in a digital age, have been greatly reduced. Individuals are able to launch micro-businesses from home, with the aid of digital technology, in a way that was not previously possible. Therefore, many markets are now crowded with a multitude of vendors.

Globalization has also led to an increasing number of suppliers in many markets. The fall of the Berlin wall on 9 November 1989 opened up eastern Europe, with many of its countries now competing with the rest of the world.[14] The growth of countries in Asia, most famously India and China, has also led to increasing competition in many areas of business.[15] Whereas before the world wide web, sourcing appropriate suppliers, even locally, could be a challenge, people can now source vendors globally with relative ease.

Everything in life has a cause and effect; nothing exists in a vacuum. The direct effect of living in a world with an abundance of information is that attention has now become scarce. Today, we have so many entities vying for our attention. We are constantly reacting to phone calls, texts, e-mails and social media messages, etc. The 'Internet of Things' means even our cars, fridges and boilers are increasingly communicating with us and sending us information! We are so 'plugged in'. The Canadian sociologists, Anabel Quan-Haase and Barry Wellman coined the term 'hyperconnectivity' to describe this phenomenon.[16] For example, the average text message is responded to within 90 seconds;[17] now that is a hyperconnected world! Moreover, the explosion of media means we are constantly catching up on apps, blogs, messaging services, social platforms and online digital radio, TV and video channels as well as still utilizing many traditional media.

With more demands on our attention than ever before, it is harder for any one person, business or organization to engage us. In fact, in order to manage all this information, we are personalizing as much as possible. In so doing we try to cut out the irrelevant material for which we simply have no time. Of course, digital enables this to happen. From the news we read, to the music we listen to and the programmes we watch, we are increasingly personalizing our own experience.

A consequence of this is that some of the traditional ways in which serendipity played a part in our lives are disappearing. Many of us no longer flick through a multitude of channels when there is nothing to watch, an occasion when we may have stumbled across a new programme which we really enjoyed. Instead, we are choosing specific programmes on catch-up TV online.

Increasingly, we tend to only listen to the music we really like, with many radio stations playing songs from a very particular era or genre. Even when digital services recommend new music, it is from a very narrow selection based on previous listening. Certainly, many of us are less exposed to the variety of sounds previously pumped out by stations trying to cater to a more diverse group of listeners.

In some cases, this even means we are not hearing as many different voices and opinions on current events. Many people prefer to filter the news through particular apps, blogs or digital offerings that take a particular view and purvey the world in a certain way. For example, services such as Apple News, launched in September 2015, are designed to aggregate the news specifically to your interests,[18] in other words, the global news just for you.

This personalization of the world we inhabit has become increasingly necessary for us to be able to deal with the amount of communications and information to which we are exposed on a daily basis. Quite simply, without filtering and cutting out so much that we deem irrelevant, we could not cope with the copious amounts of material constantly coming at us.

This scarcity of attention, and the increasing personalization of our experiences, has serious ramifications for the world of sales.

For many people in sales, generating their own leads has always been a big part of their job. This lead generation has often been achieved, metaphorically speaking, by 'bashing down doors'. Cold calling potential prospects, either by literally knocking on doors or more usually these days via the phone, has been a major way of creating sales opportunities for multitudes of salespeople for decades, but this whole approach is becoming increasingly ineffective.

Practically, it is becoming harder and harder for salespeople to break through the technological ecosystem that exists around any potential prospect. Whereas there was a time when many office employees were based at their desk and regularly answered their work phone, this is no longer the case. Companies are more flexible, with individuals working more varied hours, hot desking and, at various times, operating from home. Phone calls go through to voicemails, while e-mails are missed or ignored amongst the infinite number that many people receive daily. Simply getting through is a harder task than in any previous era.

However, the challenge is a deeper one. If, years ago, a salesperson did get through, and the prospect did have some interest in the products or services they were offering, they may well have agreed to a face-to-face meeting. In a world where accessing information was difficult, spending an hour with a salesperson may have been the most efficient way of learning about the market. In this way a fair value exchange took place. The person selling obtained some face-to-face time, where they might be able to secure a deal at some point in the future. The prospect gathered a little market intelligence and knowledge they did not have previously.

Today, with the abundance of information available, this value exchange no longer works. While salespeople still want to get in front of prospects in order to try to realize a sale, buyers no longer feel the requirement to see a salesperson in order to learn about a market. A face-to-face meeting is generally too much time given over to one supplier early in a buying journey. It is often deemed less convenient than researching online, which can be undertaken 24/7 and usually at less precious moments in the day, in terms of utilization of time. For example, one may undertake research on a train on the way to or from work, in a few moments of downtime or during an evening or weekend.

Traditionally, people tolerated unexpected sales calls either in person or by phone. Although they were often an inconvenient and irrelevant interruption, there were occasions when they provided value. Today, we are less tolerant. Safe in the knowledge that as customers we have been empowered to find the products and services we require at a time of our choosing, we are less inclined than ever to respond favourably to these approaches.

For those in selling, the consequences of this are twofold. First, salespeople are generating fewer leads using these traditional channels than in the past.[19] They are becoming less effective, as prospects who do not see value in the approach no longer agree to meetings in the numbers they did before the digital age.[20]

Second, prospects are less tolerant of advances made in this way. In a world where people are personalizing their experiences, irrelevant and unsolicited calls, messages or e-mails seem much more intrusive than they once did.[21] Is the best way to approach a potential customer to irritate them by trying to get their attention in a manner they find invasive?

Moreover, we previously lived in a world where it was not always easy to access suppliers. Therefore, if they came to us at an appropriate time, we were often willing to engage. Today, we can connect with an array of providers of products and services whenever we like, and so our perception of those approaching us is less favourable. We will often view them as desperate or being a lesser-quality vendor – hence, perhaps, their need to call us speculatively. If our automatic disposition is to think less well of these companies, and individuals, it is not a great way for a salesperson to start a dialogue with the hope of winning a customer.

So, the traditional lead-generation model utilized by salespeople all over the world is not an effective one for the digital age. This immediately renders the sales funnel, which has been utilized since the tail end of the 19th century, redundant.[22]

Figure 1.1 Traditional Sales Funnel

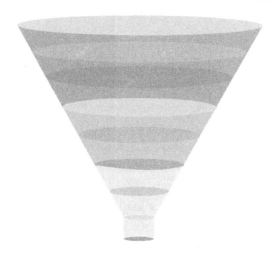

This is because the top of the sales funnel worked on volume. The idea was to reach a lot of people, most of whom would not be interested in your offering. However, those who were, became active prospects. They would then be taken through a buying journey and some would become paying customers. These customers provided your return on investment (ROI). As long as the customers who came out of the bottom of the funnel paid for all the activities at the top and through the funnel, with some profit on top, the sales function was deemed to be successful. In other words, the idea was to start with many prospects. These would steadily reduce in number until they were whittled down to the paying customers that emerged from the bottom.

However, it is very difficult for salespeople today to generate the sort of volume they require merely from cold calling. With the use of technology and the increasing mobility of the workforce they are simply not having enough conversations using these methods. Moreover, fewer people are willing to be taken on the customer journey, opting to go through much of it themselves without the need for a salesperson to be involved at all.

This renders the traditional sales funnel useless as a model and a measure. Prospects are no longer entering the sales funnel at the top to be guided through it by the salesperson. Instead, buyers are creating their own processes and utilizing a multitude of resources including websites, blogs, forums, review sites and social media platforms, etc. With so much choice, information and options, customers are forging their own path. Salespeople once had the knowledge buyers required. Now people can access that information whenever they choose. The power has increasingly shifted away from the company to the customer.

That the direction of travel is increasingly one in which buyers undertake much of the purchase journey themselves, makes complete sense. Social proof has always had the most influence on human behaviour; that is, what others say and do. This is the reason why word-of-mouth recommendations and referrals have always been the best route to market for any company. As purchasers, we trust the views of 'other people like us' more than anyone else. In the old analogue world, we would often rely on word of mouth, but there may have been occasions when we didn't get the opportunity to ask the opinion of others. There may also have been times when we were making buying decisions relating to products or services about which our immediate network had no experience.

In a world in which everyone has a channel, however, word of mouth has now gone online. As culturally social platforms increasingly become the communication medium of choice for a growing number of the population, it is becoming progressively easier to see what family, friends, colleagues and the wider community think about any particular product or service. For most people, when it could be accessed, word of mouth was always the most reliable route to market. The 'social web' has made it perennially accessible. 'The wisdom of friends', as Sheryl Sandberg, the COO of Facebook expressed it, is increasingly becoming a reliable and influential resource in the purchase journey.[23]

Before the digital era, most information was disseminated via official channels. For example, most people would find out the news from newspapers, radio and television. When looking for new products or services, individuals would rely on the Yellow and Business Pages, trade magazines and company brochures. In other words, the majority of the information we consumed was created and distributed through official media.

In a world where everyone now has a channel, this is no longer the case. Increasingly, information is propagated via conversation and social sharing.

For example, during the Egyptian Uprising in 2011, much of the information about the happenings on the ground came from regular individuals via Facebook rather than journalists.[24] Similarly, it was a passer-by, Jim Hanrahan, who first shared the story with the rest of the world of US Airways flight 1549 landing in New York's Hudson River.[25] He broke the story a mere four minutes after it occurred. Likewise, when two bombs exploded at the Boston Marathon on 15 April 2013, it was on Twitter that the story was first reported.[26]

You do not have to be a citizen journalist, however, to utilize the power of social platforms. As we increasingly obtain our news from these digital channels, official announcements are increasingly being made on these networks, as social sharing becomes a reliable and fast way of distributing news and information.

So, for example, on 16 November 2010, Clarence House decided to break the news of Prince William's engagement to Catherine Middleton on Twitter.[27] The couple then continued this tradition by announcing the birth of Prince George in July 2013 on the British Monarchy Facebook page.[28]

Even when stories do not break on social media, the power of social sharing means that it is the way an increasing number of people find out. For example, although the Press Association were the first to disclose the story of the death of Margaret Thatcher to its subscribers, it was a tweet put out by ITV News, one minute later, that informed the wider public of the event.[29]

With the abundance of information available, buyers are undertaking their own research online without the requirement to engage with salespeople. Of course, prospects will access official channels such as company websites. However, these are often less trusted sources than forums, review sites and social media comments, where people can access the 'wisdom of friends' and utilize word of mouth, which is traditionally most people's channel of choice.

Social sharing, whether it is for news, sport, entertainment or information about products and services, is becoming a major source of knowledge on which people increasingly rely. In fact, according to GlobalWebIndex's research in January 2015, 28 per cent of all web activity is spent on social platforms.[30] That means that for every five minutes spent online, one minute and fifteen seconds is on social platforms. Moreover, they are being used to inform buyers. Global research provider Nielsen reported that 46 per cent of people surveyed in late 2011 said they turn to social media when making purchasing decisions.[31]

Social platforms, of course, are only a part of the digital story. When one considers that buyers are also using websites, forums, review sites and blogs, the influence that digital media is having on procurement is unfathomable. For example, a study undertaken by Research Now in 2014 suggested that blogs have a major influence on buying outcomes, with 84 per cent of people having undertaken a transaction based on a blog at one time or other.[32] In terms of digital generally, a B2B procurement study undertaken by Acquity Group, owned by Accenture, reported that 94 per cent of B2B buyers search online when making purchasing decisions.[33]

However, prospects are not undertaking only their initial research online. Buyers are completing an increasing amount of the purchase journey before they have any direct contact with a potential supplier. After extensive research, the Corporate Executive Board reported in 2012 that the average buyer is 57 per cent of the way through the purchase journey before even accepting direct contact with a salesperson, and it can often be much more.[34]

This has severe ramifications. The later in the buying journey that salespeople get involved, the harder it is to influence the purchase. In fact, increasingly, buyers will identify their own requirements and leave salespeople to deal with procurement departments only interested in obtaining the best possible terms. This is often achieved by playing suppliers off against one another, on a standard set of purchase criteria. Of course, in this scenario the salesperson has had no chance to differentiate their offer or demonstrate further value. Therefore, each supplier is treated as a mere commodity.

This situation also has implications for any sales meeting that does take place. Salespeople have to ask themselves where they add value. Obviously, from their own company's point of view, they contribute with the sales they make. More importantly though, where is the value from the customer's viewpoint? Credibility is not neutral. If a customer has a meeting with a salesperson they do not know, then during the encounter they will form a more positive or negative view of that individual from the one they had when the interaction began.

It is unlikely that a buyer will purchase from a salesperson they see in a negative light. If a salesperson goes into a meeting and merely regurgitates all the material that can be accessed from the web, then, having not obtained any new information, the prospect is most probably going to see the meeting as a waste of time. That being the case, the person selling will have very little credibility whatsoever, and it will be less likely that they make a sale.

In fact, the position is often worse, because many salespeople are still relying on some form of consultative or solution-based selling, whereby they ask a lot of questions, identify the pains and challenges the prospect has and then suggest appropriate solutions.[35] But what if the customer has already gone through much of the purchase journey themselves? What if they have already identified the pains and the solutions they think are most appropriate?

In this increasingly likely scenario, the salesperson does not add value but instead frustrates the buyer by taking them through a process that they perceive they have already undertaken. When individuals have so much knowledge at their fingertips, merely providing standard information is pointless. Going into sales meetings looking to identify needs and provide solutions is a conversation that many prospects don't want to have.

In many ways, good selling has never changed. Salespeople give value when they influence the customer's criteria of purchase. In the days when buyers had very little access to knowledge, salespeople could influence a prospect's criteria of purchase by merely explaining how their company operated. With little market intelligence, before the meeting, buyers would start formulating their ideas based on the information the salesperson provided.

As buyers became more sophisticated, in many markets, it was not enough for a salesperson to merely tell them how their company operated. Osmosis and word of mouth meant prospects had a basic understanding of various sectors. Therefore, salespeople had to apply their knowledge to the customer's situation. By identifying where the challenges were and tailoring their solutions to the buyer's situation, salespeople created value by assisting in the formulation of the buying criteria.

Today, with more of the purchase journey being completed alone, prospects are increasingly obtaining the information, recognizing their challenges and identifying the solutions without the need for engaging suppliers. For a salesperson to go through this process again, will often be deemed a waste of time by the customer.

In order to give value, though, salespeople still need to influence the buyer's criteria of purchase. However, the way this is achieved is different. If a salesperson enters the prospect's buying journey later in the process, then the only way to do this is to challenge some of the assumptions the buyer has already made.

Certainty isn't persuadable.

In other words, if a salesperson reinforces the assumptions a buyer has already made, then from the prospect's perspective, the salesperson has provided no value. They will also not have given the customer any reason to take action, especially with them. At best, the salesperson will be seen as simply another provider like all the others, and will therefore be severely challenged on price and other terms of business, if they even get the deal at all.

So in order to influence the buyer's criteria of purchase, a salesperson has to challenge the conclusions that the prospect has already reached. Of course, not every aspect of their decision making will be questionable or need to be queried. By giving even a little 'insight', that makes the buyer reassess their own thoughts, a salesperson will have provided value and influenced the buying criteria of the customer. By 'insight' we mean that 'aha moment'. That brief instant where a new piece of knowledge or consideration is introduced into a person's cognition.

For example, I was witness to a sales meeting where a well-known retailer was commissioning a new building project. They were seeing various architectural practices to choose one to oversee the project. They had already identified their criteria of purchase and the meeting was conducted more like an interview than a traditional sales situation. At one point the buyer asked if the architectural firm had a certain amount of insurance cover. It was a rather pedestrian question. The retailer had asked it more to tick the box than anything else. Apparently, there is a standard amount for which most commercial architects, working with big retailers, are covered and the expectation was that these experienced firms would all have the same.

The architect concerned indicated that not only did he have the prerequisite amount of cover, but in fact, their firm had considerably more. They had worked on one particular project where an increased amount was required. Knowing about the particular work to be undertaken, he raised the possibility that in fact the increased amount would also be appropriate in this instance.

In this example, the buyer acknowledged that the architect had made an interesting observation. The buyer had the 'aha moment'. The architect had managed to change the buyer's criteria of purchase. This had many implications.

First, the architect was instantly more credible with the buyer. They had managed to add real value to the process by providing 'insight' which actually led to a small change in buying criteria. At this juncture, that architect would have been perceived as extremely knowledgeable and someone who could really contribute if a working relationship was established.

Moreover, once the buying criteria were re-evaluated, that particular architectural firm was now the only supplier able to meet the new standards required for a purchase to be made. Of course, the buyer was likely to go back to other possible suppliers and ask them to meet this new requirement. Undoubtedly, many would be able to accommodate the new demands. However, for a while, our architect was the only game in town. Moreover, it was their firm being used as the benchmark that other practices had to match.

Obviously, the more powerful the insight, the greater the effect it will have on the purchaser. The more the new knowledge transforms the buying criteria, the bigger the influence the salesperson can have on shaping the new requirements. This creates the opportunity for the salesperson to increase their credibility, be perceived as adding real value, differentiate their offering and, therefore, have a better chance of obtaining the deal.

Of course, it may not always be possible for the salesperson to 'disrupt' the buyer. However, the more expertise a salesperson has, the more likely it will be that they will be able to make an observation, or ask a question, that forces the buyer to rethink some of their purchase criteria. Without affecting the purchasing requirements upon which the buyer has already decided, it will be very difficult for a salesperson to differentiate their offering or demonstrate any additional value.

We can ascertain that the digital economy has affected the customer in two critical ways. First, customers no longer respond to the unwanted advances of salespeople trying to sell their wares. Cold calling and other interruptions are less effective than ever before. Second, customers are inviting salespeople into the sales process much later than in previous generations, if they welcome them at all. Consequently, it is harder for salespeople to influence the buyer's criteria of purchase and in so doing increase their credibility, add value and differentiate their offering.

Of course, there are no easy answers, but the facts point to an obvious conclusion. Salespeople used to be able to influence the criteria of purchase because it was difficult for buyers to access information.

In this scenario, it was often efficient for a purchaser to meet with a few salespeople. After a few meetings, the customer would have a good idea of the market and the most appropriate solution. Their views would have been shaped by the conversations they had with salespeople.

In many ways, nothing has changed. Salespeople still need to be present in the places where customers are learning and formulating their buying decisions. This is happening less in face-to-face meetings as purchasers use websites, blogs, forums and social media platforms to obtain information and make purchasing decisions. Therefore, salespeople have to be present and engage with prospects, at this juncture and in those places.

Moreover, if buyers are less likely to respond to cold calls and other interruptions, surely salespeople have to try to get in front of prospects in another way? If purchasers are increasingly formulating their decisions while surfing online, then evidently, this is where salespeople should be engaging and generating leads.

Salespeople cannot afford to sit idly by and continue to be cut out of the sales process. Instead, they have to get involved at the point at which customers are searching and formulating ideas. This means 'digital selling' is now upon us.

Increasingly, the time between thought and action is diminishing. For example, sitting in a bar, a friend recommended that I check out a book they had recently read. Years ago, that would have meant going to the bartender and asking to borrow a pen. I would then have had to write down the name of the book on a napkin and put it in my pocket. When I got home, I would have had to ensure I hadn't forgotten why I had the napkin and accidentally thrown it away. I would then have to remember to go into my local bookstore the next time I was in the high street, and take a look at the title my friend suggested.

In reality, I immediately went online and searched for the book, whereby a picture of the cover came up. I showed my friend, who indicated that was indeed the right volume at which point I bookmarked the page to look at later on. Of course, I could have even bought the book then and there. Today, we are used to immediate gratification. I have access to the web 24/7 and can get an instant response to almost anything.

This means that many buying journeys start 'in the moment'. That is, at the very instance a suggestion is made or a thought pops into the customer's mind. There is now very little time lag between the customer having the purchasing idea and then starting the quest of gathering intelligence to make the decision. The implication is that salespeople need to build their presence online so they are found at the moment their prospects are looking and learning.

Interestingly, although the purchasing journey may start immediately, it is in fact longer today than ever before.[36] One reason given for this is that customers have much more choice and access to information than previously. On important purchases, they therefore have the opportunity to examine more options in detail. Moreover, according to a February 2015 McKinsey report, today there are now more influencers and decision makers involved in the purchasing process.[37] Perhaps this is because it is now easier for more people to access information online and make cursory judgements, whereas years ago they would have to participate in many more meetings that time would prohibit. With more individuals involved, buying decisions are likely to take longer.

With a more protracted purchasing journey taking place, salespeople have an opportunity to influence prospects. If they ensure they have presence and partake in conversations where buying selections occur, that is on social platforms, forums, blogs etc., then they have a chance of determining purchase decisions as a longer research and evaluation process is likely to be undertaken.

As customers' buying habits increasingly change, salespeople have to react appropriately. Failure to do so will lead to missed deals. Embracing the developments, however, could lead salespeople to new and exciting opportunities. The world of digital selling is upon us. It is up to salespeople to grasp the moment in order to remain relevant and successful.

Endnotes

1 Colossus, first computer: (undated) The Colossus Computer, *The National Museum of Computing* [online] http://www.tnmoc.org/explore/colossus-gallery [accessed 22 November 2015]

'Colossus Mk 1 was delivered to Bletchley Park in late December 1943/ January 1944, was assembled there by Harry Fensom and Don Horwood, and was working in early February 1944. Colossus was the first of the electronic digital machines with programmability, albeit limited in modern terms.'

2 First message via ARPANET: Suzanne Deffree (2015) ARPANET establishes 1st computer-to-computer link, *EDN Network*, October 29, 1969, published 29 October [online] http://www.edn.com/electronics-blogs/ edn-moments/4399541/ARPANET-establishes-1st-computer-to-computer-link–October-29–1969 [accessed 22 November 2015]

'The first message on the ARPANET was sent by UCLA student pro- grammer Charles S Kline at 10:30 pm on October 29, from the campus' Boelter Hall to the Stanford Research Institute's SDS 940 host computer.'

3 Growth of the Internet: Barry M. Leiner, Vinton G. Cerf, David D. Clark, Robert E. Kahn, Leonard Kleinrock, Daniel C. Lynch, Jon Postel, Larry G. Roberts and Stephen Wolff (undated) The initial internetting concepts, *Internet Society* [online] http://www.internetsociety.org/ internet/what-internet/history-internet/brief-history-internet [accessed 22 November 2015]

'The original ARPANET grew into the Internet... By 1983, ARPANET was being used by a significant number of defense R&D and oper- ational organizations... by 1985, Internet was already well established as a technology... and was beginning to be used by other communities for daily computer communications.'

4 First web page: (undated) History of the web – Sir Tim Berners-Lee, *World Wide Web Foundation* [online] http://webfoundation.org/about/ vision/history-of-the-web/ [accessed 22 November 2015]

'Tim also wrote the first web page editor/browser (WorldWideWeb.app) and the first web server (httpd). By the end of 1990, the first web page was served on the open internet, and in 1991, people outside of CERN were invited to join this new Web community.'

5 Royalty-free www: (undated) History of the web – Sir Tim Berners-Lee, *World Wide Web Foundation* [online] http://webfoundation.org/about/ vision/history-of-the-web/ [accessed 22 November 2015]

'...Tim and others advocated to ensure that CERN would agree to make the underlying code available on a royalty-free basis, forever. This decision was announced in April 1993, and sparked a global wave of creativity, collaboration and innovation never seen before.'

6 Broadband Independent: Kate Youde (2010) Broadband: The first decade, *Independent*, published 28 March [online] http://www. independent.co.uk/life-style/gadgets-and-tech/news/broadband-the-first-decade-1929515.html [accessed 22 November 2015]

'Telewest launched home ADSL – asymmetric digital subscriber line, as it was known – in the UK on 31 March 2000, with Goldsmith Road in Gillingham, Kent, the first street to receive the technology after the trial at Mr Bush's home.'

7 Six Degrees: Michael Ray (2014) Social media – early pioneers, *Encyclopedia Britannica*, published 27 June [online] http://www. britannica.com/topic/social-network [accessed 22 November 2015]

'SixDegrees.com was the first true social networking site. It was launched in 1997 with most of the features that would come to characterize such sites: members could create profiles for themselves, maintain lists of friends, and contact one another through the site's private messaging system.'

8 Social media in early 2000s small business: Drew Hendricks (2013) Complete history of social media: then and now, *Small Business Trends*, published 8 May [online] http://smallbiztrends.com/2013/05/ the-complete-history-of-social-media-infographic.html [accessed 22 November 2015]

'MySpace and LinkedIn gained prominence in the early 2000s, and sites like Photobucket and Flickr facilitated online photo sharing. YouTube came out in 2005... By 2006, Facebook and Twitter both became available to users throughout the world. These sites remain some of the most popular social networks on the Internet.'

9 LinkedIn: (undated) About LinkedIn: Company information, *LinkedIn* [online] https://press.linkedin.com/about-linkedin [accessed 22 November 2015]

'LinkedIn started out in the living room of co-founder Reid Hoffman in 2002. The site officially launched on May 5, 2003. At the end of the first month in operation, LinkedIn had a total of 4,500 members in the network.'

10 Facebook: (undated) Facebook history, *Facebook* [online] https://www. facebook.com/notes/286498461501332/ [accessed 22 November 2015]

'Facebook was founded on 4th February 2004 by Mark Zuckerberg with his college roommates and fellow Harvard University students Eduardo Saverin, Andrew McCollum, Dustin Moskovitz and Chris Hughes.'

11 First iPhone: (undated) Apple's iPhone in pictures, *Telegraph: Technology online* [online] http://www.telegraph.co.uk/technology/apple/iphone/5477324/Apples-iPhone-a-history-in-pictures.html [accessed 22 November 2015]

'The first ever iPhone was unveiled by Steve Jobs... in January 2007. Its limited functionality in its early days – including not being able to connect to the internet independently of WiFi – meant it was effectively an entire computer that happened to make phone calls.'

12 BBC: (undated) British Broadcasting Corporation, *Encyclopedia.com* [online] http://www.encyclopedia.com/topic/British_Broadcasting_Corp.aspx [accessed 22 November 2015]

Encyclopedia.com records that in addition to BBC1, BBC2 was launched in April 1964. In July 1967, BBC2 started to broadcast in colour. *In the same year, 'In keeping with the enhanced broadcast capabilities of the VHF system, the BBC introduced a fourth radio network in 1967 that was devoted to popular music and named it Radio 1. The existing networks became Radios 2, 3, and 4, respectively.'*

13 BBC after 2000: (undated) British Broadcasting Corporation, *Encyclopedia.com* [online] http://www.encyclopedia.com/topic/British_Broadcasting_Corp.aspx [accessed 22 November 2015]

'In 2007, the company operated ten channels...including BBC3, BBC4, CBBC, Cbeebies, and BBC News 24... BBC is also the largest operator of radio stations in the United Kingdom, with more than 35 stations, including Radio 1, 1Xtra, Radio 2, Radio 3, Radio 4, and Five Live.'

14 Berlin Wall: Gabriele Suder (2009) Fall of the Berlin Wall: A victory for Europe, *Bloomburg Business*, published 5 November [online] http://www.bloomberg.com/bw/stories/2009-11-05/fall-of-the-berlin-wall-a-victory-for-europebusinessweek-business-news-stock-market-and-financial-advice [accessed 22 November 2015]

'The transition to market-based economies in most Central and Eastern European countries created significant opportunities for markets, resources, supplies, and manufacturing. We saw a huge increase in cross-border trade and foreign direct investment.'

15a Growth of Asia Greater Pacific Capital: (undated) India: Where China was 10 years ago, not all emerging markets are the same? *Greater Pacific* [online] http://greaterpacificcapital.com/india-where-china-was-10-years-ago-not-all-emerging-markets-are-the-same/ [accessed 22 November 2015]

'India Central to Asia Pivot. Asia is a critical growth region in the world today... home to 60% of the global population, represents 34% of global GDP, 34% of global market capitalisation and 40% of global trade... expected to account for 55% of global economic growth by 2050.'

15b Growth of Asia Greater Pacific Capital: (undated) India: Where China was 10 years ago, not all emerging markets are the same? *Greater Pacific* [online] http://greaterpacificcapital.com/india-where-china-was-10-years-ago-not-all-emerging-markets-are-the-same/ [accessed 22 November 2015]

'This economic shift has also been accompanied by a political one, with the Western world paying increasing importance to China's growing influence in South Asia.'

16 Hyperconnectivity: (undated) Definition of hyperconnectivity, *Dictionary* [online] http://lexbook.net/en/hyperconnectivity [accessed 22 November 2015]

'The term refers to the use of multiple means of communication, such as email, instant messaging, telephone, face-to-face contact and Web 2.0 information services. Hyperconnectivity is also a trend in computer networking in which all things that can or should communicate through the network will communicate through the network.'

17 SMS: Expert Commentator (2013) SMS marketing campaigns, *Smart Insights*, published 23 September [online] http://www.smartinsights.com/mobile-marketing/sms-marketing-campaigns/ [accessed 22 November 2015]

'98% of text messages are read, with the average response time a mere 90 seconds (compared to 2.5 days for an email)'

18 Apple News: Joe Rossignol (2015) Inside iOS 9: Apple News delivers the latest stories to your device, *Mac Rumours*, published 16 September [online] http://www.macrumors.com/2015/09/16/inside-ios-9-apple-news-app/ [accessed 22 November 2015]

'Apple News all-new app on iOS 9 that aggregates stories from several sources into one mobile-friendly format for reading on iPhone, iPad and iPod touch... very similar to news apps such as Flipboard and Zine, displaying a list of news articles and personalized stories based on publications that interest you.'

19 Traditional channels: Meghan Lockwood (2013) The ultimate resource for 2013 inbound marketing stats and charts [SlideShare], *Hubspot*, published 20 May [online] http://blog.hubspot.com/marketing/2013-inbound-marketing-stats-charts [accessed 22 November 2015]:

'*#83 – Inbound marketing delivers 54% more leads into the marketing funnel than traditional outbound leads.*'

20 Telesales/cold calling less effective: John Jantsch (undated) The abusive math of cold calling, duct tape marketing [online] http://www.ducttapemarketing.com/blog/the-abusive-math-of-cold-calling/ [accessed 24 December 2015]

'*Cold calling results in about a 1–3% success rate for getting an initial appointment and it's generally abusive to both parties.*'

21 Unsolicited calls: Barbara Giamanco and Kent Gregoire (2012) Tweet me, friend me, make me buy, *Harvard Business Review*, published July–August [online] https://hbr.org/2012/07/tweet-me-friend-me-make-me-buy [accessed 9 October 2015]

'*...the return on cold calling is dropping with every passing year. Indeed, in a recent survey by InsideView, an online provider of sales-relevant content, more than 90% of C-level executives said they "never" respond to cold calls or e-mail blasts.*'

22 Sales Funnel: Mark Bonchek and Cara France (2014) Marketing can no longer rely on the funnel, *Harvard Business Review*, published 7 May [online] https://hbr.org/2014/05/marketing-can-no-longer-rely-on-the-funnel [accessed 22 November 2015]

In this article, *the Harvard Business Review* asked companies such as Google, SAP, Twitter and Visa to assess the relevance of the marketing funnel. The article cites a typical online experience whereby, in response to a social media or e-commerce site's recommendation, the purchaser can go from awareness to consideration and ultimate purchase within just a few moments. The report makes the point that in both B2B and B2C, people are researching online, with colleagues and with friends, thereby finding their own way through the funnel and exiting, ready to make a purchase. They found that, '*In both B2B and B2C businesses, customers are doing their own research both online and with their colleagues and friends. Prospects are walking themselves through the funnel, then walking in the door ready to buy.*'

23 Wisdom of friends: Donna Tam (2012) Facebook COO: Search to harness the 'wisdom of friends' *CNet*, published 1 October [online] http://www.cnet.com/news/facebook-coo-search-to-harness-the-wisdom-of-friends/ [accessed 22 November 2015]

This report from CNet.com quotes Sheryl Sandberg, the COO of Facebook: '*When you're looking for information, the question is who do you want it from? Do you want it from the wisdom of crowds or the wisdom of friends?... if I'm looking for a restaurant to go to, I'd rather get a recommendation from a friend.*'

24 Egyptian uprising: Sam Gustin (2011) Social media sparked, accelerated Egypt's revolutionary fire, Wired, published 2 November [online] http://www.wired.com/2011/02/egypts-revolutionary-fire/ [accessed 22 November 2015]

'*Facebook definitely had a role in organizing this revolution,*' *Ali told Wired.com. 'It acts like an accelerant to conditions which already exist in the country. Twitter and YouTube serve as amplification for what's happening on the ground. And they directly affect Western media coverage.*'

25 US Airways 1549: Claudine Beaumont (2009) New York plane crash: Twitter breaks the news, again, *Telegraph*, published 16 January [online] http://www.telegraph.co.uk/technology/twitter/4269765/New-York-plane-crash-Twitter-breaks-the-news-again.html [accessed 22 November 2015]

'*Twitter users broke the news of the incident around 15 minutes before the mainstream media alerted viewers and readers... The first recorded tweet came from Jim Hanrahan, four minutes after the plane went down, who wrote: "I just watched a plane crash into the hudson riv [sic] in manhattan."*'

26 Boston bombings: Andrew Kirell (2013) The very first tweet about the Boston Marathon bombings... *Mediaite*, published 15 April [online] http://www.mediaite.com/online/the-very-first-tweet-about-the-boston-marathon-bombings/ [accessed 22 November 2015]

'*With a timestamp of 2:50 pm ET (the exact moment the first explosion occurred), this woman's tweet was the first "report" on what turned out to be a terrifying ordeal at the marathon: Kristen Surman @KristenSurman Holy shit! Explosion! 11:50 AM - 15 Apr 2013.*'

27 Royal engagement: (2010) Clarence House @clarenceHouse, *Twitter*, published 16 November [online] https://twitter.com/clarencehouse/status/4489951894835200 [accessed 20 November 2015]

'The Prince of Wales is delighted to announce the engagement of Prince William to Miss Catherine Middleton – www.princeofwales.gov. uk.11:04 AM – 16 Nov 2010.'

28 Birth of Prince George, Daily Mirror: Ann Gripper (2013) News of birth of royal baby born in social media age announced on Twitter, Instagram, Facebook and Google Plus, *Mirror*, published 22 July [online] http://www.mirror.co.uk/news/uk-news/news-birth-royal-baby-born-2079184 [accessed 22 November 2015]

'The press release… was posted on The British Monarchy Facebook page. It said: "Her Royal Highness the Duchess of Cambridge was safely delivered of a son at 4.24pm." The baby weighs 8lbs 6oz. The Duke of Cambridge was present for the birth.'

29 Mrs Thatcher press: William Turvill (2013) Press Association reveals Thatcher death news and ITV News is first to break it on Twitter, *PressGazette*, published 8 April [online] http://www.pressgazette.co.uk/press-association-reveals-thatcher-death-news-and-itv-news-first-break-it-twitter [accessed 22 November 2015]

In this article, William Turvill reported that the news of Margaret Thatcher's death was first circulated by the Press Association following a call from her spokesman Lord Bell. However, he reveals that it was ITV's Twitter feed, @ITVNews that broke the news to the general public at 12.48 pm – no less than a minute after the Press Association issued their own newsflash. Lord Bell's statement said: *'It is with great sadness that Mark and Carol Thatcher announced that their mother Baroness Thatcher died peacefully following a stroke this morning. A further statement will be made later.'*

30 GlobalWebIndex: Shea Bennet (2015) 28 per cent of time spent online is social networking, *Adweek*, published 27 January [online] http://www.adweek.com/socialtimes/time-spent-online/613474 [accessed 22 November 2015]

'How much time do you spend each day on social networks? According to new data, the average user logs 1.72 hours per day on social platforms, which represents about 28 per cent of all online activity.'

31 Social media influence: Masroor Ahmed (2015) Is social media the biggest influencer of buying decisions? *Social Media Today*, published 31 May [online] http://www.socialmediatoday.com/marketing/masroor/2015-05-28/social-media-biggest-influencer-buying-decisions [accessed 22 November 2015]

'Quite simply, social media is a peer influencer when it comes to making buying decisions, as 71% of consumers are likely to purchase an item based on social media referrals.'

32   Research Now – blogging: (2014) Big on blogs – study of 1,000 finds that 84 per cent of people buy products based on the content of a blog (Infographic) *Research Now*, published 24 November [online] http://www.corporate-eye.com/main/the-influence-of-blogs-on-purchase-decisions/ [accessed 22 November 2015]

- *'84% of people buy products based on the content of a blog, and one in four people buy something monthly.*
- *People are more put off by paid content than they are by advertising.*
- *45% of people have contacted a blogger to ask a question when considering purchasing a product.'*

33   Acquity report: (2014) 2014 state of B2B procurement study, *AccentureDigital* [online] https://www.accenture.com/il-en/insight-state-b2b-procurement-study-uncovering-shifting-landscape.aspx [accessed 22 November 2015]

- *'94% of B2B buyers report that they conduct some form of online research before purchasing a business product.*
- *55% of B2B buyers conduct online research for at least half of their corporate purchases.*
- *40% of buyers research more than half of goods under $10,000 online.'*

34   CEB report 2012: (2013) Think with Google: B2B's digital evolution, *ThinkWithGoogle*, published February [online] https://www.thinkwithgoogle.com/articles/b2b-digital-evolution.html [accessed 22 November 2015]

'Today's business buyers do not contact suppliers directly until 57 per cent of the purchase process is complete. The challenge for marketers is to be present in these channels at all times with content that educates buyers and helps guide commercial decisions.'

35   Consultative selling: Brent Adamson, Matthew Dixon and Nicholas Toman (2012) The end of solution sales, *Harvard Business Review*, published July–August [online] https://hbr.org/2012/07/the-end-of-solution-sales [accessed 22 November 2015]

In this article from *Harvard Business Review*, the authors write that the days of sales reps specializing in discovering customers' needs and selling them solutions only worked when customers did not know how to solve their own problems, but now, 'solution sales reps' are more of an annoyance than an asset and buyers are often way ahead of the salespeople who are helping them. The report goes on to reveal: *'a recent Corporate Executive Board study of more than 1,400 B2B customers found that those customers completed, on average, nearly 60% of a typical purchasing decision – researching solutions, ranking options, setting requirements, benchmarking pricing, and so on – before even having a conversation with a supplier.'*

36 Purchasing journey: Fiona Briggs (2014) Savvy shoppers now make over nine visits to a retailer's site before deciding to buy, Rakuten Marketing finds, RetailTimes, published 25 November [online] http://www.retailtimes.co.uk/savvy-shoppers-now-make-nine-visits-retailers-site-deciding-buy-rakuten-marketing-finds/

'Today, Rakuten Marketing attribution data reveals shoppers are no longer making impulse purchases, with the average customer making 9.5 visits to a brand before buying. This is an increase of seven visits since January 2011, when shoppers visited just 2.5 times before converting.'

37 McKinsey report: Oskar Lingqvist, Candace Lun Plotkin and Jennifer Stanley (2015) Do you really understand how your business customers buy? *McKinsey and Company*, published February [online] http://www.mckinsey.com/insights/marketing_sales/do_you_really_understand_how_your_business_customers_buy [accessed 22 November 2015]

'... an explosion of communication vehicles and interaction channels has ratcheted up the expectations of business purchasers. Many more influencers and decision makers are now involved in the purchasing process, and business buyers too have been shaped by their consumer shopping experience. As a result, their behaviour has become more consumer-like.'

How the sales role changes in a digital environment   02

The real power of a brand is in the 'mindshare' it obtains. For example, if I ask you to think of three soft drinks, there is a good chance that Coca Cola would be one of the products that comes to mind. Similarly, if I ask you to consider some luxury cars, Mercedes and BMW would be two manufacturers that would be likely to appear.

These companies have paid for this 'mindshare' over many decades. The power of these brands is that if a purchaser is thinking of buying a soft drink, Coca Cola will often be one of the products that is considered. Likewise, if someone were in the market for a luxury car there is a good chance that Mercedes and BMW will be in their buying set. To be able to get a 'seat at the table' whenever someone is in the market for the product or service you supply, delivers incredible business opportunities. This, of course, is why an established brand is worth so much. In essence, it brings in a number of sales in its own right.

The word brand is derived from the Old Norse word *brandr* which means to burn.[1] It refers to producers burning their mark on the products they made in order to differentiate between them. Modern branding, as we understand it today, emerged from the rise of mass production.[2] As goods started to be produced in volume, companies were selling beyond their immediate locality, but it was difficult to compete with local suppliers whose products were known by the community in a region.

Therefore, products were packaged in a way that made them identifiable. The promise these 'brands' delivered could then be communicated to customers in order to win their trust. Branding, in essence, was a way of differentiating a product. It represented a promise to the customer so they knew exactly what to expect.

Branding has rightly been seen as a marketing discipline and so it could seem out of place in a book about selling. However, in the digital world, branding has become important for salespeople. In fact, the reality is that it has become important for everyone. The social web has turned every individual into a media personality. This is not to be confused with fame. Fame suggests being known by many people. Although the world wide web makes it easier for everyone to be known by more people than ever before, that is not what I am referring to.

Being a personality is different. It refers to the fact that our lives are more open and transparent than in any previous era. Traditionally, it was only celebrities who would have many aspects of their existence known by strangers. Today, various facets of our beings are accessible to anyone who has an interest in looking.

It means that whether it is a job interview, a date or a business meeting, people have the ability to find out about you before a face-to-face encounter occurs. In fact, there are a variety of different types of software and apps that assist in this endeavour. For example, Charlie App[3] will search through hundreds of online sources and send you a one-page summary on anyone you are going to meet. By looking at the pictures you post, the connections you have, the information you disseminate and the comments you make, people will formulate an opinion about you; in other words, an expectation of what you are like. In marketing terms this would be your brand promise.

Everyone today is managing their own personal brand, in a way that was unheard of before the world of social platforms and digital media. Today, everyone is a brand manager, creating a certain perception and expectation of who they are before a direct encounter ever occurs.

As customers progressively go online to find out about products and services, decide buying criteria and make purchasing decisions, salespeople need to ensure they have a presence in these places.[4] As has always been the case, salespeople need to be where their customers are. This is increasingly on digital platforms.

The revolution we have witnessed is that today, everyone has a channel. Increasingly, people are using these channels to communicate and disseminate their opinions. This 'social proof', whether in social networks, forums or on blogs, then influences the purchasing journeys of others.

Salespeople, therefore, need to make use of these channels. It is imperative that salespeople have a blog, utilize the social media platforms that their customers use, and engage with their target audience within the networks, forums and communities in which they participate. They need to have a presence where the purchasing journey normally starts, and where many of the buying decisions are made.

Although digital platforms provide the opportunity for people to own their own channels, they are simply a distribution mechanism. The real currency online is content, that is, what you put on those channels. The British Broadcasting Corporation (BBC) is just a set of cables with a licence to broadcast. What makes it a well-respected organization is the content it produces and distributes. Similarly, without salespeople generating interesting articles, podcasts, videos and comments, the channels open to them are useless.

Producing interesting content and making insightful comments provides salespeople with the opportunity to build credibility and trust within their market. In the digital world, customers have been empowered. Their first point of reference, when looking for a new product or service, is not to open up the Yellow or Business pages and call a company with the hope of learning more about what is on offer. Rather, in the first instance, they will go online and undertake their own research.

The challenge for salespeople is that having undertaken their research, many of the criteria of purchase will have been formulated before a salesperson has any chance to influence the prospect. In fact, being invited to the later stages of the buying process might be as good as it gets for many salespeople. As purchasers conduct research and, most likely, narrow down their buying set to a few suppliers, most companies won't get any opportunity with the customer at all. However, what if a salesperson can start to influence this journey by having a presence in the places the customer undertakes their fact finding?

When people are making a purchasing decision they will be influenced by the information they encounter online. It is this material that creates the opportunity for a salesperson to engage with, and influence, a buyer early on in their purchase journey. In fact, the content can affect the prospect even before the salesperson knows they are in the market to buy.

By producing some of the media with which a buyer interacts, a salesperson gets to influence the purchasing journey before a customer makes contact with them directly. Moreover, by creating content that the prospect finds valuable, the salesperson will be perceived as knowledgeable and, therefore, credible. This is a first step in earning the customer's trust.

When a prospect approaches a salesperson because they have engaged with some of their content, or been impressed by their comments, it provides a number of advantages. They already see the salesperson as credible, having obtained some value from them even before any direct interaction takes place, and so are probably more open minded and more willing to enter into a meaningful conversation with that salesperson. Moreover, because it was the prospect making the approach, rather than the salesperson bashing down their door, they do not perceive the salesperson as being desperate. In other words, the exchange that is entered into is between equals.

Finally, in a world where people are time poor, it is highly probable that any person who makes direct contact with a salesperson is likely to be in the market to buy. In other words, interactions are more likely to take place when the prospect is seriously considering a purchase. Generally, when salespeople approach prospects, even when they are interested, the timing is often less than perfect. Keeping the lead 'warm' can take a considerable amount of effort and adds an enormous amount to the cost of sale. This can be expected to be significantly reduced when it is the prospect making the first contact.

Therefore, a substantial part of lead generation today is about salespeople creating a presence in the places their prospects and customers frequent. Salespeople are no longer the sole providers of information enabling buyers to make a purchasing decision. Customers are now defining their own journeys in any acquisition they make. Producing content of value, answering questions, and participating in forums enable a salesperson to engage with prospects. In so doing, when the prospects are ready to buy, that salesperson becomes one of the suppliers they are likely to contact. This can all be tested and measured, as will be explained later, in Chapter 5.

This approach has profound implications for the way sales and marketing work together. Traditionally, direct interaction with customers was the dominion of the sales department, and so lead generation channels such as cold calling and door knocking were often left to the sales team. Marketing would then utilize other routes to market where interpersonal interaction would not take place, such as direct mail, advertising and producing supporting material like leaflets and brochures, etc. Although both departments may have produced leads, there was usually a clear demarcation between the channels being used.

These clear lines are now completely blurred. Marketing departments are normally responsible for websites and utilizing other digital platforms such as social media and blogs. Therefore, the marketing team are producing and commissioning content and distributing it online.

However, salespeople have now become mini marketing entities working in similar channels, commenting on posts and even, at times, producing content of their own. Of course, a simple approach would be to question whether a salesperson needs to undertake activities already being performed by marketing. There is, though, a fundamental difference. The marketing department's concern is with promoting, enhancing and building their company's reputation. Salespeople are first and foremost augmenting their own credibility; the organization necessarily comes second.

This approach is essential in the 'experience economy' that we have now entered. Increasingly, people are no longer buying products or services but 'experiences'.

Before World War Two, we were a product economy.[5] The overwhelming majority of commerce was in the manufacturing, distribution and purchasing of products. Differentiation between items was, in relative terms, easier to achieve than in our modern economy, as choice was much more limited. Moreover, the speed to market was slower than it is today, and when a company did create a unique aspect to their offering, they may have had significant time to capitalize on that advantage before the competition caught up.

In this environment, the conventional wisdom was that salespeople should concentrate on selling the benefits of a product as opposed to features that may not immediately resonate with a customer. For example, during the 1930s a feature promoted by Procter and Gamble for its Ivory Soap was that it was a purer soap.[6] The benefit to the customer was smoother hands, rather than the rough skin which people often got from frequently washing the dishes.

After World War Two, as the western industrialized world grew richer, products started to become ubiquitous and, therefore, commoditized.[7] This led to companies creating services around products in order to enable them to be differentiated.[8] In retail, this presented itself through stores offering services such as free delivery, extended warranties and money-back guarantees. In business, companies such as IBM started to see themselves as service providers rather than manufacturers of hardware.[9] This allowed IBM to take a more consultative approach, selling tailored hardware solutions to meet the challenges its customers were facing.

It is easy to see how the idea of consultative, or solution, selling grew out of this situation. Customers were unaware of the different options available to them when making a purchase. Before the web, accessing this information would not be easy. A salesperson would meet a prospect and question them about their current situation and challenges, and having done so, they could recommend a specific product, or tailored service, to meet the customer's requirements.

In the web-enabled world, this model has now changed; customers have been empowered to undertake the diagnosis themselves. With the amount of information available 24/7, customers can get a long way down the purchase journey before a salesperson is involved. Therefore, many customers no longer want to have what they perceive as a pedestrian conversation, once deemed necessary to the consultative sales approach.

Moreover, in the same way that products became commoditized, making it necessary for companies to provide services around their offering, services today have become a commodity. As the western industrialized economies have grown, and become ever-more sophisticated, services have come to dominate. With the majority of businesses defining themselves as service providers, there is now little differentiation between most companies in any given sector.

This does not mean service is not important. As products became commoditized, we still expected them to work. In fact, as companies competed for our business we demanded that their goods improve. Similarly, we still require excellent service. In reality, we hold companies up to higher standards today than ever before, as businesses fight for our custom. However, it is becoming increasingly difficult for companies to differentiate themselves simply by the services they offer.

Today, it is not the making of products or the delivery of services that will enable companies to differentiate themselves. Rather, it is the creation of experiences that provides businesses with the opportunity to stand out. We will explore how businesses differentiate themselves in the experience economy in Chapter 5.

The move to experiences, though, is not simply to enable companies to differentiate themselves. It is because it is being demanded by customers. A fundamental difference between a service and an experience is that a service is done 'to' you, whereas an experience is done 'with' you.

So, for example, I have always found that Amazon delivers an excellent service. Of course, I have to order an item, but once I have, I go through an automated process where everything is done to me. On the other hand, a sporting event such as the World Cup Final or Super Bowl is not done *to* the spectator but *with* them. This is because the sense of occasion is not simply delivered by all the star players, coaches and managers showing up. It also requires 70–80,000 fans to attend. Imagine the Super Bowl, World Cup Final or any major sporting occasion without the crowd. The players would still be vying for the same trophy, but the sense of occasion would just not be comparable. In other words, the audience is part of the event. They contribute to delivering the sense of occasion, and so it is not done to them but with them. Of course, sporting events are not new, but there are fundamental reasons why customers are increasingly choosing experiences over mere service.

In a world where everyone has a channel, we are becoming less passive and taking a more participatory role in the activities that we undertake. For example, television is increasingly becoming a two-screen experience, with people using tablets and smartphones to enhance their viewing. According to Nielsen, 84 per cent of smartphone and tablet owners use these devices when watching TV.[10] Similarly, business conferences are progressively incorporating the use of a second screen.[11] This is to involve delegates, encouraging them to post comments, ask questions and take polls of their views during the course of the day. In this way, enterprises that used to be very passive are becoming more active affairs.

As more time is spent online, the web itself is not a passive medium. Whereas the phrase 'couch potato'[12] was coined to refer to someone who sits on the sofa and watches TV all day, the phrase 'web potato' has not been used in the same way. Both are sedentary activities requiring little physical exertion, but it does not seem fitting to call someone a 'web potato'. Generally, we would deem someone who watches TV all day lazy, due to the fact that it seemingly requires no effort whatsoever on their part. However, the web is not a passive activity. It requires us to click, comment and take action in a way that TV does not. Quite rightly, we don't perceive surfing the web as being inactive.

Digital technology and the web have resulted in us being less passive in so many aspects of our lives. Social media has encouraged people to share opinions and comment about events in a way in which we were not previously accustomed. The accessibility of information has empowered people to check out facts, research arguments, take control of purchase journeys and generally be less reliant on the word of a few individuals. In addition, digital allows us to personalize more of our world, just to suit us. From catch-up TV to music streaming, the daily news to personalizing products, we are continually encouraged to make active choices. For example, Nike allows customers to design their own trainers rather than accept the 'off the shelf' design to which we were all once restricted.[13]

As a society, our values are also changing. So many of our possessions used to be symbols of status and success. Of course, there are times when this is still the case but it is less so than in previous generations. There are a number of reasons for this development.

For one thing, products have become better and more accessible. From laptops to smartphones and cars to clothing, in almost every price bracket there are quality products available. In other words, the differential between the haves and have nots, in terms of material possessions, is far less than in previous generations.

Moreover, so many of the products that we once bought have been condensed down into software. For example, people would buy a quality leather diary and address book, invest in a nice watch and pay for a good camera. These items are all now standard fare on a smartphone. In their homes, people would make features of their extensive music or book collections. Nowadays, for an increasing majority of the population, these things are accessed as software on a smartphone. In fact, I used to own a compass, calculator, maps and a Dictaphone, all of which I now access from my smartphone. In many ways we simply don't need as many 'things' as we once did.

All this points to a world where there is increasingly more utility in what you do than in what you own. This is compounded as social media and messaging services have become the dominant form of communication.[14] Taking a picture of your new watch and sharing it with your network might come across as bragging. However, taking a picture from an important sporting occasion, an interesting event, a global landmark or even having fun with friends is perceived not as showing off, but rather sharing what you are doing and letting others into your world. Maybe part of this is because the watch is only about you, whereas the event is normally seen as bigger than just an individual.

These trends affect the world of business to business as much as the consumer market place. In many ways the purchase journey has already become more of a customer experience. Buyers are much more actively involved in seeking out information and options, rather than simply relying on a few visits from some sales reps.

The importance of salespeople in differentiating between features and benefits came out of the product economy. Consultative or solution selling emerged from the service economy. It is now disruptive or insight selling that is required in the experience economy.

Features and benefits were necessarily all about the product. When customers did not have easy access to information it was salespeople who educated them and influenced their criteria of purchase. The focus of the meeting, however, was on the product itself.

As products became commoditized, it was the bespoke services that became the differentiator. By asking questions, 'consultative selling' enabled a salesperson to understand a customer's situation, and in so doing, tailor the services for that individual. By making suggestions and recommendations from the suite of services they could offer, a salesperson would affect the customer's criteria of purchase. The focus of the meeting would be on the tailored solutions the customer required.

Today, services are a commodity. Prospects have already diagnosed the challenges they have, and solutions they require, before they speak with a salesperson. In order, therefore, for a salesperson to influence the criteria of purchase, they need to 'disrupt' the customer's paradigms. By providing 'insight' and giving a customer an 'aha' moment, they may alter the perception an individual has of their reality, and change the customer's requirements of purchase. This 'insight' may lead to a small change in the customer's perception or have a bigger impact. The important factor is that it enables a salesperson to provide value and in so doing, be seen as a credible partner.

In this scenario, the differentiator is not the product's benefits and features, nor the tailored services, rather it is the 'insight' provided. In other words, in today's selling environment, the differentiation is often not created by 'what' is being sold but by 'how' it is being sold. In a world where products and services are often the same, it is the experience that is distinct. In a sales situation, this experience is delivered by the salesperson.

Ultimately, in order to add value, salespeople have always had to influence the criteria of purchase the customer has. In the product economy, this would be achieved by simply explaining the product in terms of benefits to the customer. In the service economy, this was accomplished by 'meeting the needs' of the customer through tailoring the services offered. In both examples the salesperson was 'serving' the customer and differentiating by the offering.

However, in the 'experience' economy, the offering may be irrelevant, inasmuch as it may not be very different from the competition. The differentiator becomes the 'experience provided' which, in a sales situation, is the salesperson. By delivering real 'insight', and therefore tangible value, the company is positioned, through the salesperson, as not merely being a supplier but a real partner who can add genuine value to the customer. Thus the 'sales experience' itself becomes as important as the product or service being sold.

Creating this experience, though, does not start in the meeting. In fact, if it is not delivered earlier, the face-to-face encounter may never happen. This experience begins with the customer's initiation of the buying journey, so a necessary part of selling and lead generation today is for salespeople to use the relevant channels in order to build their personal brand. In this way, they become more visible, establishing credibility and eliciting trust. Prospects and customers alike will perceive them as a significant person within the market. By utilizing the appropriate social platforms and media channels at their disposal, with insightful and interesting content, salespeople enhance their reputation and begin the process of influencing the purchasing decision.

As salespeople deliver value and enhance their reputation in any particular market place, the real value of a brand will start to come into play: 'mindshare'. Within finite markets, if salespeople become active in relevant platforms, forums and blogs then they can become known as a valuable and knowledgeable voice within the sector, and individuals will become aware of them. When someone is ready to buy, that particular salesperson may be one of the people or resources they check. In other words, just like Coke, Mercedes and BMW have 'mindshare', so too will the salesperson within their particular industry.

The difference, however, is stark. Big brands 'paid' for mindshare. Through advertising on billboards, in magazines and on radio and TV etc., many of us could not help but know these companies because they ensured they were in front of us frequently. We had no choice but to recognize them. Today, mindshare does not have to be bought but can be 'earned'. If a salesperson creates content of value, prospects and customers will interact and share the material. Therefore, when the prospect is ready to buy, the salesperson will already be known and may be one of the resources they choose to use. Similarly, if colleagues are in the market for a particular product or service, the salesperson may be one of the people recommended.

Of course, producing this content, and commenting and contributing to forums and blogs etc., takes time and effort, and therefore, de facto, costs money. However, we refer to it as mindshare 'earned' because the recognition comes from prospects and customers choosing to interact with the media being produced. 'Paid for' mindshare is when I see your advert, regardless of whether I want to or not. It's very ubiquity makes it almost impossible to ignore. 'Earned' mindshare is when the content being produced is utilized out of customer choice.

By salespeople having a presence, and creating content of value in the places their customers start their buying journey, mindshare can be earned. This, in turn, enables salespeople to get into the buying set of their prospects when they are ready to buy. In so doing, they are able to generate qualified leads from individuals who are serious potential customers.

This means that Sir Francis Bacon's old adage 'knowledge is power'[15] is no longer true in the world of selling. Once it was indeed the case, because salespeople would have knowledge that prospects required in order to make buying decisions. A prospect would see a salesperson in order to obtain that knowledge.

Today, information is ubiquitous. Buyers no longer perceive they need to see a salesperson at the beginning of their purchase journey in order to comprehend the market place. A salesperson who takes the view that 'I have the knowledge and if the customer meets me I will impart it' will probably never get in front of the customer.

Rather, today, 'shared knowledge is power'. In other words, if salespeople utilize their media channels to share insight and knowledge, in the places their customers look, they will provide value and be seen as credible. Consequently, mindshare can be earned and when the customer is ready to engage, the salesperson will be one of the suppliers considered. Having knowledge doesn't generate leads. It is the sharing of knowledge that creates business opportunities.

Of course, in this environment, companies worry about competitors obtaining information, awareness and intelligence that they may not otherwise have had. Obviously, a company does not have to share everything online. If something is particularly sensitive or secret, then it can be held back from general view.

While there will be occasions when guarding knowledge, information and expertise will be appropriate, most of the time, holding material back will do more harm than good. In a world of abundance of information, it has become a commodity. The general perception of a prospect is that if they don't get the knowledge from you, they will get it somewhere else. In the main, this is in fact the case. Therefore, sharing expertise attracts potential customers to your business; keeping it secret does not.

Moreover, we live in a fast-paced and transparent world, where people interact with a multitude of individuals and share material with ease. In this setting, keeping secrets and knowledge 'under wraps' becomes increasingly challenging. Sometimes, the best way of safeguarding information is to publish it and be able to prove you were the creator of the idea. This is an alternative to trying to keep the material guarded, and risking others sharing the intelligence first. Once they have, you have lost the opportunity of taking credit for bringing the concept to the market.

In a scenario where the salesperson and their insights will be a major differentiator in winning the business, one can see that while marketing concentrates on raising the company's reputation, salespeople are necessarily enhancing their own position first and the organization's second. Both marketing and sales can be utilizing similar channels, with the same ultimate goal, to increase sales and revenue into the business. However, the methods of achieving this will be different.

Of course, this could work well if integrated and organized properly. It can also be a recipe for disaster if handled in the wrong way. This is why sales and marketing must now work so closely together. This is a challenge I address directly in the Epilogue.

Just as marketing departments use content to win the attention of prospects and build the reputation of the business, salespeople are doing the same. Whereas marketing departments may be doing this on a macro level, salespeople may be working in tighter market segments, and at times addressing particular individuals.

By doing this, salespeople become a 'brand'. That is, the contributions they make and content they publish allows them to differentiate themselves from others in the field. By having a public persona, salespeople will create a perception and expectation among customers: 'the promise' if you like. This may be done inadvertently, but the best salespeople will plan it strategically. Either way, the outcome is the same. Salespeople now have to concern themselves with managing 'brand me'. In fact, becoming known, and being seen as credible and trustworthy, is vital to creating a useful online presence.

Today, when everyone has a channel, the very nature of branding has changed. Previously, branding was all about image, in other words, what a company portrayed about itself. Businesses would come up with logos and designs to stand out from the rest of the market. The images and words used were there to convey exactly what the business stood for and its promise to customers. In a world where, in the main, it was only those who could afford to pay who could take advantage of media, it was companies themselves that delivered their message. Image was all important and all encompassing.

Of course, image is still important today. The way a company communicates and depicts itself is vital. This will, of course, be true for an individual salesperson as well. However, when everyone has a channel, there is something even more important than image, and that is reputation. Whereas image is what a company says about itself, reputation is what others say.

Word of mouth is the most powerful route to market because social proof – what others say and do – is the biggest influencer on human behaviour. In a world where everyone has a channel, word of mouth is increasingly going online. Of course, this does not negate the word of mouth that exists offline, but utilizing digital platforms, customers are increasingly sharing information, posting positive and negative comments about products and services and making recommendations to each other that can be accessed by all. Top review sites such as Amazon, Trip Advisor and Yelp can influence buyer behaviour even when we don't know the individual reviewers.[16] This is as true for business-to-business review sites and forums as it is for hotels, restaurants and books.

It is imperative that salespeople utilize this digital media. To ignore one of the major resources customers use to make purchasing decisions would be a dereliction of their role. Once salespeople are online, then managing their own reputation becomes important.

Salespeople need to be proactive about reputation management. This means that every time they deliver for a happy customer, the salesperson should be asking for a testimonial. Gone are the days of receiving a letter, or even an e-mail, from a customer expressing their delight at the product or service they have purchased. Of course, these are flattering to receive but are of little help in building a positive reputation online.

Rather, salespeople should be asking customers to post positive comments on public platforms such as Twitter, Facebook, LinkedIn and Google+ etc. Of course, many customers may choose not to post anything, nor should a salesperson hassle them to do so. However, if salespeople continually ensure that they always ask, at the appropriate moment, then these testimonials will build up. In addition, by linking them all back to a testimonials page on a blog, for example, salespeople are also giving themselves more of a chance to be found when a search is undertaken. If day after day, week after week, month after month and year after year salespeople continually encourage satisfied customers to post positive endorsements, cumulatively this will have an extremely positive impact over the course of time.

Of course, not everything that is being written about a salesperson, either good or bad, may have been requested, so salespeople should be constantly monitoring what is being said about them, and their products and services, online. In order to be able to manage their reputation properly, salespeople have to be aware of everything that is being authored. Social media monitoring software such as Mention,[17] Hootsuite[18] and Sprout Social[19] will allow salespeople to receive alerts when keywords such as their name or product are quoted.

Digital platforms do not work the same as traditional broadcast media. These long-established channels worked one way, whereby companies paid for exposure in order to communicate a message. The receivers of the information had little right of reply. Digital is different. Everyone has a channel and, therefore, a right of response. That is why these platforms are considered 'social'. They are not simply channels where an individual or company transmits ideas and everyone else listens. The opportunity to reply is a given.

Therefore, if someone comments or responds in a positive way, ignoring them, whether deliberate or not, is quite simply rude. It is also a missed opportunity to engage a potential prospect or customer. Salespeople must have a mechanism for monitoring the remarks on these platforms.

Moreover, if negative comments are made, then by monitoring these comments, salespeople have the opportunity to respond. Of course, there will be times when the best course of action might be to ignore a comment, but some sort of response, certainly initially, is normally the right approach. This is because it demonstrates that the salesperson is paying attention, has acknowledged the prospect or customer's view, and has tried to resolve it in some way. If an ongoing dialogue or conversation is necessary then it would usually be better, after the initial response, to take it into a private forum, for example on e-mail or over the phone. Every case must be taken on its merits. Needless to say, each company and salesperson needs to take reputation management extremely seriously.

It is, therefore, vital that before posting anything online, you always consider the consequences. This means invariably looking at it from the recipient's viewpoint and not just your own. Consider whether it could be misinterpreted in any way. By having these checks in place you minimize the risks of making mistakes that could adversely affect your reputation.

Another aspect of 'reputation management' is authenticity. That is, being genuine. Obviously in all environments, whether business or personal, we will accentuate certain aspects of our personalities and suppress other character traits. There are appropriate ways to act in a particular capacity and situation, and we take these into account in the way we choose to behave.

Nevertheless, within these boundaries it is important that individuals are sincere in their interactions. In a world where companies paid for media and the recipients of the message had little opportunity to reply, images could be created that were completely fabricated. Since people didn't have access to information or proper dialogue, companies often got away with this approach.

Today, the situation is different. Information is readily available and so claims that organizations make can often be checked and verified. Conversations, exchanges and comments made online often obligate individuals and businesses to respond. In this climate, those that are fake will normally be found out. Once they are, credibility and trust are usually lost. Therefore, while salespeople may build a business persona it has to be genuine and based on reality. Authenticity is key to building a personal brand that brings success.

Salespeople have always had to build good reputations and have excellent interpersonal skills. Of course, the more stature a salesperson has, the more credible and influential they are with customers. Previously, salespeople accomplished most of their achievements in direct interactions with prospects, either on the phone or face to face. In the digital economy, it is important for salespeople to be able to translate these abilities onto online platforms.

For many years, salespeople have had to be perceived as real experts in their field. However, now they have to be able to package some of that knowledge and create 'value' that will engage prospects at the beginning of their buying journey, and before personal interaction takes place.

Salespeople have always had to come across well when face to face with a client, but now they also have to be able to communicate via other media. This can be in written articles, on podcasts or on video. In fact, all three may be required.

Finally, salespeople have always needed to be seen in good standing by their prospects and customers. In the main, we do business with people we like. Today, though, salespeople need to go further and build a brand. This will enable them to 'earn mindshare', which will lead to recommendations, referrals and enquiries. It will also allow a salesperson to build credibility and trust in order to be able to secure a meeting. While many appointments used to be secured through telephone interaction with prospects, customers today are increasingly using online platforms to discern between suppliers. Salespeople need to be able to elicit the same confidence they obtained on the phone, in an online environment and often before a personal interaction takes place. This will be achieved through the value, promise and reputation that a salesperson can convey. In other words, the 'brand' they build.

Endnotes

1 Brandr origin: Mustafa Kurtuldu (2012) Brand new: the history of branding, *DesignToday,* published 29 November [online] http://www.designtoday.info/brand-new-the-history-of-branding/ [accessed 14 December 2015]

'... Branding' comes from the Old Norse "Brandr" which means to burn. Cattle, slaves, timber... were burnt or branded with the symbols of the owner using a hot iron rod... The transition from "This belongs to me..." to "This was made by me..." started to evolve in the 1800s.'

2 Modern branding: Matt Shadel (2014) A brief history of branding, *Convoy,* published 8 Jan [online] https://www.weareconvoy.com/2014/01/a-brief-history-of-branding/ [accessed 14 December 2015]

'The 1820s saw the rise of mass production... producers began burning their mark into cases of goods to distinguish themselves... Over time, the brand evolved into a symbol of quality rather than ownership... In 1870, it became possible to register a trademark to prevent competitors from creating confusingly similar products.'

3 Charlie App: Charlie [online] https://charlieapp.com/ [accessed 14 December 2015]

4 Buying decisions: Kimberlee Morrison (2014) 81% of shoppers conduct online research before buying [Infographic] *Adweek,* published 28 November [online] http://www.adweek.com/socialtimes/81-shoppers-conduct-online-research-making-purchase-infographic/208527 [accessed 14 December 2015]

'Eighty-one per cent of shoppers conduct online research before they make a purchase. Sixty per cent begin by using a search engine to find the products they want, and 61 per cent will read product reviews before making any purchase.'

5 Product to service economy: Jeremy Black (2011) Overview: Britain from 1945 onwards, *BBC History,* published 3 March [online] http://www.bbc.co.uk/history/british/modern/overview_1945_present_01.shtml [accessed 24 December 2015]

'Uncertain public policy in the post-war period played a role in the marked relative decline of the British economy, which was particularly pronounced in the field of manufacturing... Manufacturing decline was matched by the rise in the service sector, resulting in a major change... in the experience of work.'

6 Procter and Gamble: (undated) Ivory Product History, *P&G* [online] https://www.pg.com/en_CA/product_card/pb_ivory.shtml [accessed 14 December 2015]

'*Harley Procter... wrote the slogan "99-44/100% Pure: It Floats." This became a pledge of quality to Ivory consumers.*'

7 Industrialized world: (undated) Paradoxes of global acceleration 1945 – present, *World History for Us All* [online] http://worldhistoryforusall. sdsu.edu/eras/era9.php [accessed 14 December 2015]

'*Since 1950, the global economy has grown faster than ever before in history. Indeed, by some measures, more economic growth has occurred in this era than in all previous eras of human history combined.*'

8 Adding value: Werner Reinartz and Wolfgang Ulaga (2008) How to sell services more profitably, *Harvard Business Review*, published May [online] https://hbr.org/2008/05/how-to-sell-services-more-profitably [accessed 14 December 2015]

'*Manufacturers frequently believe that adding value in the form of services will provide a competitive advantage after their products start to become commodities.*'

9 IBM: Henry Blodget (2012) IBM's a software company now! *Business Insider,* published 21 August [online] http://www.businessinsider.com/ ibm-software-company-2012-8 [accessed 14 December 2015]:

'*... IBM customers still buy mainframes – but mainframes are now a tiny portion of IBM's business... IBM reinvented itself as a services business. For more than a decade, IBM's resurgent growth was driven by a global services organization that implemented and managed global-scale IT and business services for corporations and government.*'

10 Nielsen: (2014) What's empowering the new digital consumer? *Nielsen Newswire,* published 2 October [online] http://www.nielsen.com/us/en/ insights/news/2014/whats-empowering-the-new-digital-consumer.html [accessed 14 December 2015]

'*Eighty-four percent of smartphone and tablet owners say they use their devices as second screens while watching TV... Consumers use second screens to deepen their engagement with what they're watching, in-cluding activities such as looking up information about the characters and plotlines, or researching and purchasing products and services advertised.*'

11   Conference second screen: Chris Cavanaugh (undated) Experience marketing forecast for 2014: it's all about engagement, Chris Cavanaugh: Second screen technology, *FreemanXP* [online] http://freemanxp.com/insights/blog/experience-marketing-forecast-for-2014-its-all-about-engagement/ [accessed 14 December 2015]

'Second screen allows for meeting, event, or consumer activation participants to drill more deeply into content, share thoughts, and ask questions. For program organizers, the analytics allow content owners to understand in real time what is resonating, where audiences are spending their time, and what questions need answering.'

12   Couch Potato: (undated) Couch Potato, *Vocabulary* [online] http://www.vocabulary.com/dictionary/couch%20potato [accessed 14 December 2015]

'It was first used by a 1970s comics artist who drew lazy, sedentary characters he called couch potatoes... the phrase became an extremely popular way to talk about someone who's spent so much time in front of the TV that he seems more like a vegetable than a human being.'

13   Nike: (undated) Mass customization: directory and reviews of customizable products, NikeiD [online] http://www.mass-customization.com/custom-shoes/nikeid/ [accessed 14 December 2015]

'Nike is one of the mainstream brands who pioneered the industry of mass customization... NikeiD was launched in 1999 and was initially offered through their online site. The first customizable shoe was the Air Force... Today, there are countless customizable shoes – from the popular basketball shoes to the classic canvas pairs.'

14a   Messaging: Luke Johnson (2012) Texts overtake calls as most used communication method, *The Gadget Website*, published 18 July [online] http://www.t3.com/news/text-messaging-overtakes-calls-as-most-used-communication-method [accessed 14 December 2015]

'James Thickett, Ofcom's director of research: "By far the most popular means of communication on a day-to-day basis is by text messaging... Talking face to face or on the phone are no longer the most common ways for us to interact with each other."'

14b   Messaging: Susan Tardanico (2012) Is social media sabotaging real communication? *Forbes*, published 30 April [online] http://www.forbes.com/sites/susantardanico/2012/04/30/is-social-media-sabotaging-real-communication/ [accessed 14 December 2015]

'In the workplace, the use of electronic communication has overtaken face-to-face and voice-to-voice communication by a wide margin.'

15 Knowledge is power: (undated) Today in Science History: Sir Francis Bacon (22 Jan 1561–9 Apr 1626) English philosopher remembered for his influence promoting a scientific method, *Today in Science History* [online] http://todayinsci.com/B/Bacon_Francis/BaconFrancis-Quotations.htm [accessed 14 December 2015]

'Knowledge is power [Editors' summary of Bacon's idea, not Bacon's wording.] – Sir Francis Bacon'

16 Buyer Behaviour: Dan Hinckley (2015) New study: data reveals 67% of consumers are influenced by online reviews, *Moz.com*, published 2 September [online] https://moz.com/blog/new-data-reveals-67-of-consumers-are-influenced-by-online-reviews [accessed 14 December 2015]

'We asked participants, "When making a major purchase such as an appliance... how important are online reviews in your decision-making?" The results revealed that online reviews impact 67.7% of respondents' purchasing decisions.'

17 Mention: Mention: realtime social media monitoring [online] https://mention.com [accessed 14 December 2015]

18 Hootsuite: Hootsuite: social media management [online]: https://hootsuite.com [accessed 14 December 2015]

19 Sprout Social: Sprout Social: social media management [online] sproutsocial.com [accessed 14 December 2015]

Preparing to go online   03

In addition to the marketing and sales functions, there are likely to be other individuals and departments making use of digital media within an organization. Customer service teams may monitor and assist purchasers via channels such as Twitter or Facebook. Company directors, as the leaders in the business, may be encouraged to communicate with relevant audiences. Finally, other employees may choose to comment and share items about the corporation for which they work; this could be with family and friends, or suppliers and customers with whom they have some interaction.

All of these departments, and individuals, should be encouraged in their use of social media. We live in a world where the most precious resource in communications today is 'attention'. The more a business has it, and therefore is front of mind when a purchase is going to be made, the greater the likelihood it will be considered as one of the possible suppliers. Companies that are talked about frequently online, and have their content shared, increase their probability of being found. As long as most of the comments and interactions that take place are overwhelmingly positive, then they should be seen as beneficial.

In order to ensure remarks are favourable to the enterprise, there has to be guidance given by the company for the messaging that is produced. It cannot be completely uncontrolled. With no guidelines, there is a danger that an ill-advised post could have detrimental effects on an organization. The other challenge, when a multitude of communications is occurring, is how to maintain cohesiveness.

This joined-up approach is vital. All companies require a strong identity. Without its prospects and customers having a clear understanding of the offering it provides, no organization is likely to win much business. Moreover, in order for a company to build a solid reputation and earn trust, customers have to feel they recognize what the company stands for and is all about. If communications are not cohesive it will be impossible for people to grasp the organization's proposition. In turn, the business will not be able to establish a good reputation and trustworthiness in the market. Quite simply, without a unified approach, an organization's media presence will just be a mess.

Essentially, it means that a company has to define its tone of voice in a way that is simple to understand, live by and impart to others. Ideally, this will be done at board level and disseminated throughout the organization. It can be the responsibility of marketing and the communications team who will then impart it to the rest of the business. Whatever the mechanism, it is vital that the tone of voice is determined and understood by everyone.

Without establishing the company's 'tone of voice', it is impossible to decide what content should be produced for the variety of platforms the business wishes to exploit. Individuals can have a plethora of ideas and suggestions. However, content is supposed to engage customers, deliver value and encourage them to interact further with the organization. Without properly defining its communication style, it is unlikely that a business will be able to create powerful content of real value. Being able to generate messages that enable a company to fulfil its own business objectives, requires a strategic approach to communications.

For example, an individual may come up with an idea to produce a series of compelling animations in order to impart useful information and engage prospects and customers. Are animations an appropriate communication device for the enterprise? Should they be funny, playful or serious? Will they create a perception of the organization that will work positively with its customer base and ultimately lead to business?

There are no right or wrong answers to these questions. Rather, it is a case of what is appropriate. Without defining the company's 'tone of voice' it will be impossible to know whether animation, in this example, is one of the approaches to use.

Salespeople, who are often the face of the business, have to be true to this tone of voice. If an organization has not defined it, then salespeople will have to get involved and assist in this endeavour.

Salespeople have to build their own personal brand. That is, they have to bring value to customers, differentiate themselves and in so doing build a good reputation within their market. Salespeople also have to determine their own 'tone of voice' before they go online. This must be done in tandem with the company and fit in with its style. If the organization has failed to define its tone, it will be difficult for a salesperson, or anyone else, to communicate effectively.

Any inconsistency across a corporation is likely to have an adverse effect on sales, as customers will inevitably receive a variety of different experiences when interacting with the business. Without consistency, a company cannot build credibility and trust. This comes from a prospect, or customer, knowing what to expect from an organization and having their positive expectations met.

Therefore, an enterprise must consider its 'tone of voice' before it goes online. A company's tone of voice is made up of three distinct parts, all of which will be explored in detail. These are:

1 the ethos or purpose of the business;

2 the core deliverable or value proposition;

3 the emotional selling proposition.

1. The ethos or purpose of the business

It is no coincidence that three considerable providers of personal cloud computing services, with similar offerings, appeared within a few months of each other. Google Docs was started in February 2007[1] and Microsoft's Windows Live SkyDrive[2] was released in August 2007. Meanwhile, although Dropbox[3] was not officially launched until 2008, the company was started in June 2007.

Similarly, when two other major players entered the personal cloud storage market they did so within a few months of each other. Amazon launched its Cloud Drive in March 2011[4] and Apple's iCloud joined the others in June of the same year.[5] Of course, this also ignores the many other companies that were, and are still, providing other cloud-based solutions.[6] The point is that whereas many companies used to be able to differentiate and stand out simply by 'what' they did, in most market sectors, this is no longer the case.

We used to live in a world where there was very little choice in the market. Moreover, before the web, it was not always easy to access that choice. Prospects would identify a few possible suppliers and opt for one that could satisfy their requirements at an acceptable price.

The speed of commerce was slower. Companies that created completely new offerings, or produced innovations on existing products and services, would often have a relatively long time before their competitors brought the same developments to market. These days, first-mover advantage is extremely limited. In an economy where speed provides a competitive edge, other suppliers will look to emulate the offering, in order to level the playing field, as quickly as possible.

The nature of communication has also changed. Most marketing, in essence, was transactional. Magazine and newspaper advertising, catalogues and brochures, direct mail and leaflet drops etc., were mainly used in order to elicit a response from a prospect.

For example, a business would take the time to design a direct mail. It would be printed and sent to a particular database. Once it left the organization, however, that piece of mail had no inherent value for the company. The only worth it had was in the responses that it generated. The same could also be said for the recipients. Statistically, most would throw the mailer away because they did not regard it as having any importance. Those few prospects or customers who responded to the communication would most likely capture the company's details in whatever database or address system they used and then dispose of the direct mail. In other words, the only purpose of the correspondence was to elicit a response. There was no other point from the viewpoint of either sender or recipient.

A lot of advertising on radio, in cinemas and on television was also used in the same way. Having invested in these channels, companies would be looking to achieve an immediate increase in enquiries and, in turn, business. Of course, it should be noted that organizations have also used mechanisms such as billboard advertising, radio and TV simply to build brand awareness. Communications designed only to strengthen a brand, without any measure of response, have normally been a luxury utilized by companies with larger marketing budgets.

Whichever routes to market a company chose, the majority belonged to media organizations. Marketing departments did not own the channels themselves. They simply paid for space, during a particular programme, or in a specific newspaper or magazine. Essentially, they spent their budget to interrupt the viewer or reader when they knew their attention was focused in a particular place.

While many of us have fond memories of particularly brilliant print adverts or TV commercials, the majority of the promotional material we received was not especially engaging. However, in a world where we had little access to choice and information, we would often pay attention to these communications.

At a time when accessing information was not as easy as it is today, culturally we relied on sales and marketing to supply us with some of our knowledge. For example, before the web, people would often choose holidays by visiting travel agents and picking up brochures. These brochures, however, were not put together by the government in order to enhance the well-being of the nation; instead, they were a means of marketing, created by companies wanting to sell holidays. Yet in a world where there was a lack of other resources, we relied on them to make decisions about our vacation; we didn't even call and ask the companies to send the brochures in the mail. Rather, we would drag ourselves down to the shops, in our own time, in order to pick up this literature!

Salespeople would also utilize direct communication channels, either over the phone or face to face. Of course, the point of these exchanges was to secure a deal, albeit that it might take several contacts for this to be achieved.

Essentially, a majority of the communications were centred around directly eliciting responses, and securing transactions, in a world where products and services were the focus of most marketing promotions and sales conversations. This was at a time where there was more likely to be 'differentiation' around 'what' the company supplied.

In this scenario, it was not essential for an organization to stand for anything more than what it offered. I am not suggesting that there were not any companies for which a greater ethos or purpose existed, and in any era of commerce that would be positive, but it was not a prerequisite in order to enable a business to become successful.

Today the landscape has completely changed. It is becoming increasingly difficult for organizations to differentiate simply by 'what' they do. Most company offerings, in the overwhelming majority of market sectors, are the same. One area, however, where a business has the opportunity to differentiate itself from others, is in its 'purpose'; in other words, 'why' it does what it does.

When customers have so much choice, this 'ethos' can be an unmistakable variance and provide a very different emphasis in a corporation's communications. The 'purpose' itself will attract individuals, thus making something other than price distinctive between company offerings.

Moreover, the web has made the world more transparent. It is easier to extrapolate a greater amount of information about suppliers, from the material that is accessible, than ever before. With so much choice available, many customers require more than just a good product or quality service. Increasingly, individuals demand that organizations hold the same values as they do. This being the case, when a purpose aligns with a particular group of customers' beliefs and values, it can enable an enterprise to 'win' business and 'retain' its clientele over a long period of time.

For example, the declared purpose of Innocent is to 'make natural delicious food and drink that helps people live well and die old'.[7] Of course, this will resonate with many individuals straight away. It is likely to get them more excited than a competitor that makes drinks that are equally as good, but with no obvious aim other than to make money.

However, it goes further. A company that declares a purpose has to have a mechanism for it to be fulfilled. Without this in place, there is a danger that the business will simply be paying lip service to a purpose it has no intention of achieving. In the transparent world in which we live, it is probable that this would be discovered somewhere down the line. At that point the company could very well be ruined. It would certainly be extremely damaging.

Innocent do have a mechanism. It declares that everything Innocent makes will always be '100% natural, delicious and nutritionally net-positive, so people are physically and mentally better off after they have eaten our food than before'.[8]

In other words, when a company has a purpose, it also affects 'how' it delivers its product or services and the promise it makes to customers. Differentiation doesn't necessarily come from what the business produces. For example, there are other companies making smoothies, but their motivation for supplying drinks, and how they are produced, can be very different because of the purpose of their business.

When a company is very explicit about its purpose, the people it attracts, both in terms of customers and employees, tend to be those who have similar beliefs and values. These are individuals with whom the purpose particularly resonates. This, then, becomes a virtuous circle, as these people live by and underpin the values of the organization; the purpose and values are strengthened, thus attracting more like minds.

In this way, you can have two or more enterprises producing smoothies. Although the product itself may appear similar, the purpose, and therefore 'how' the drinks are delivered, could be very different. This naturally influences the company's communications and, in turn, the people it attracts. The end result is that the products may be alike, but the organizations and their customers are distinct. Of course, there is room for a number of suppliers in most markets, many of which will attract contrasting customers.

Creating this difference makes it easier for a business to target the right prospects. It makes it more likely that customers will be loyal, and so improve retention figures. It also means price becomes less of an issue. Of course, cost is always a question if it is the only apparent differential between offerings.

Just as organizations need to have a purpose, so do salespeople. It enables them to appear bigger than simply wanting to get the next deal. A salesperson who seems to be willing to say anything, simply to secure the transaction, will often fail, as that will usually come across to a customer. Having a higher purpose is a way that a salesperson can bring integrity into their role, both for themselves and the person with whom they are dealing. It allows them to have a meeting of minds with customers that share the same values. This makes it easier for a salesperson to engender trust and credibility with a buyer. It also helps with identifying the right prospects, as those who do not share the same values are unlikely to buy from that particular individual.

In their professional work, a salesperson may adopt the exact purpose of the business, if it truly resonates. Alternatively, they may have their own purpose, but one that sits very well alongside the organization's reason for existing. Of course, even when a salesperson has a slightly different purpose from the enterprise for which they work, the two have to be completely aligned. An individual that is unable to achieve this is probably working for the wrong company.

The 'ethos' behind the business will assist a company in differentiating itself from the competition. It will also enable an organization to effectively utilize the communication tools at its disposal.

Whereas previously, corporations simply paid for space owned by others, today, every business possesses its own channels. Although websites, blogs and social media pages are seen in business terms as sales and marketing channels, in many ways they work more like traditional media than conventional marketing tools.

For example, a direct mail was a one-off communication that either captured a prospect's attention or didn't. Similarly, an advert on television would either prove effective or not, as might be the case. Essentially, these were one-off interactions with potential customers. Of course, mailers could be sent out regularly and TV commercials repeated frequently. This was so they would be remembered and also because a degree of repetition can be, in itself, a mechanism for persuasion.[9] Of course, in marketing terms it can also be expensive. However, the reality was that people did not buy the newspaper or magazine, or watch the TV programme, to see your advert. Rather, they saw your advert because they had chosen to watch a specific show or read a particular title.

Just like a television station or a magazine, a website, blog or social media page is only as good as the content it provides. In addition, since people have to specifically choose to visit your website, access your blog or click on your particular social media page, these new channels are quite different from past marketing formats. Previously, media organizations would create content that would attract audiences. Marketing would then pay for a small amount of the audiences' attention. Whether it is a website, blog, social media page, etc., a company now has to attract the audience itself. One way of achieving this is in the same way as a traditional media organization did: by creating great content of value.

In other words, whereas businesses simply 'paid' for mindshare, today many online marketing channels require a company to 'earn' mindshare. That is not to say that 'earning' mindshare doesn't cost money: it does. What it means is that whereas companies once paid to have access to someone else's audience, today the most effective organizations build their own audience. This is achieved in exactly the same way as is accomplished by media companies: create great content that people want to access.

Similarly, whereas salespeople generated leads purely transactionally, by making cold calls and knocking on doors, now salespeople can also build an audience of prospects within the niche markets in which they work. The 'mindshare' they will earn will achieve two objectives. Firstly, when someone is looking to buy, and in some way they are already engaged with the salesperson, that sales rep is likely to receive an enquiry. Moreover, word-of-mouth recommendations will increase, as those engaged with the salesperson may refer them even when they themselves are not in the market to buy.

If the only reason a company or salesperson exists is to make money, then it is going to be hard to consistently come up with ideas that provide value for customers and prospects. Even if a company does manage to create some content that is valuable and engaging, it will struggle to encourage people to keep returning. Disparate bits of content, even when they give value, will not necessarily be compelling enough to keep people interested.

We tend to have ongoing engagement with newspapers, magazines and websites with which we identify. Essentially, we can get the news from anywhere, but people will be drawn towards companies with which their values are more aligned. Similarly, whatever a reader's interests, such as sport or music etc., they will often gravitate to websites and magazines whose general views resonate with theirs. In other words, it is not just about obtaining information, but also buying into the general ethos of the company.

This is exactly the same in business. By having a purpose behind the organization, a company will no longer simply just create and commission content of value. Rather, there will be a thinking that holds everything together and makes all the communications more cohesive and compelling.

For example, I worked with a further education college that wanted to improve its website and start to utilize social media effectively. It was a vocational college supplying courses in subjects such as bricklaying, hairdressing and catering. The college had fantastic facilities but had a challenge in terms of its reputation. It was perceived as the poor relation to a more academic college just down the road. The headmistress explained that the general feeling in the area was that gifted students went to the academic establishment, and those with less potential would come to her college. Of course, this impression was unfair and untrue. The question was: how to start altering this view?

What was going to be put on the website? Details of all the courses? Sure, these had to be somewhere on the site but this information was not going to change opinions or be especially engaging. From a social media point of view, what material could go on a Facebook page or a YouTube channel? Of course, people could come up with ideas, but which ones would engage effectively and be the start of a potential buying journey? Moreover, what would give the material a cohesiveness so all the content worked together?

One of the keys was to identify the 'ethos' or 'purpose' of the college. The headmistress, board and staff were passionate about their work. From a sales and marketing perspective, it was a question of channelling and articulating that passion.

The headmistress explained that the college should not be seen as a poor relation to the academic establishment down the road. It was just different. In particular, she was proud of the fact that 94 per cent of students left the college and went straight into work. I was astounded. That was a phenomenal statistic.

Her observation was that many people went to the academic institution down the road with little idea of their career path. At her college, if you trained to be a plumber, car mechanic or hairdresser, then clearly you wanted a chance to get a job in those disciplines. There was no point undertaking the course and then being unable to find work, and so the college made great efforts to build links with local companies and employment agencies etc., in order to ensure that people could secure a job after their course.

It took a while to reach this juncture but this, in essence, was really the fundamental belief at the heart of the college. We coined the phrase, 'this college believes "in a return on education"'. With this ethos, content became easy. We tracked down alumni in the different subjects and made very short films of their stories. These were engaging, aspirational and demonstrated tangible results of attending the college. We interviewed successful individuals from the local area, in particular vocations, about their career path and where they saw the opportunities in their industry over the next five years.

All of this content was engaging, interesting and assisted in 'selling' the college, while providing potential students with real and tangible value. There was a cohesiveness about all the content the college created. This did not come from 'brainstorming' ideas but by understanding and properly living by the 'ethos' of the college.

By creating interesting and valuable content, which students shared and utilized, the college 'earned' mindshare of its target audience and in so doing generated an increasing number of applications to undertake its courses.

Articulating its ethos allowed the college to represent something bigger than 'what' it ultimately delivered, ie courses in vocational disciplines. The content allowed it to tap in to the hopes, aspirations and goals of the audience it served. The communications were no longer about the college, they were about the students themselves. In this way, it was engaging and 'shareable'.

This brings us to the other reason why having an 'ethos' or 'purpose' is so important. It allows you not to simply create content about 'what' you do, but to articulate it within a context, which is more compelling. The communications become more about the audience than the company supplying the products or services. Inevitably in transactional marketing and sales, the literature and conversations tend to be about 'what' the business can deliver. The 'purpose' or 'ethos' allows an organization to transcend the 'what'.

This is important because, in a world where everyone has a channel, the best salespeople and marketers a company possesses are no longer its own staff. Rather, they are the prospects and customers it can engage around the business. For example, a student sending a friend a video about a particular career, with a message, 'thought you might be interested in this', is more compelling than a multitude of messages from the college itself. Social proof, what others say and do, is the biggest influence on human behaviour. In the digital world, this can be leveraged in a way that was simply not previously possible.

People, in the main, do not share material about a company and 'what' they can supply. In essence, it is boring and undifferentiated. These details only really matter when an individual is right at the point of purchase.

People share stories and narratives that are basically about themselves. The 'purpose' or 'ethos' allows a business to have a meeting of minds with a prospect. The communications are no longer about 'what' the company does, but about the shared beliefs of both the customer and supplier. In our example, students fundamentally care about getting 'a return on education'. The 'purpose' of the college is also a cause for the customer. For the audience, these communications are no longer about the college, but about students themselves. In this context, students will share videos and stories and become the most effective salespeople and marketers for the college.

Many of the world's most successful companies have an ethos or purpose that transcends 'what' they do. For example, Bill Gates' original purpose for Microsoft, back in 1977, was 'a computer on every desk and in every home'.[10] Mark Zuckerberg wants Facebook to create a 'more open and connected world'.[11] Similarly, when Ken Blanchard, co-author of *The One Minute Manager*, amongst other titles, started his organization with his wife Marjorie, one of their declared purposes was to 'drive human worth and effectiveness in the work place'.[12]

The purposes behind the above-mentioned businesses allow individuals to become involved with these companies. Their 'purpose' can be adopted, by the audience, as shared beliefs. In this way organizations can go beyond simply 'what' they deliver and create 'champions': those people who will refer, recommend and talk about a business in a positive way. This is not because they are paid to do so, rather it is because they identify with the 'purpose' of the business and it excites them.

Not every customer has to be invigorated by an organization's ethos. However, the small minority that become passionate can create a lot of attention, and social proof, by sharing content and comments with many others. For example, not everyone is passionate enough to line up for days before Apple's next product launch, but the fact that there is a vocal minority of customers who are willing to do so creates attention and publicity for the company. The social proof this elicits means others will also consider the purchase, even if they are not quite so enthusiastic about the business.

Salespeople also need to ensure they have identified their 'purpose' or 'ethos'. It is vital if they are going to be effective at using digital media to generate leads and gain referrals. By producing, commissioning and using content that articulates and fits with their purpose, they will be able to engage prospects. This will permit salespeople to 'earn mindshare' in a world where attention is so precious. Once 'attention' is obtained, salespeople can engage in conversations and start to create leads and begin the buying process with prospects. It will also allow salespeople to start establishing credibility and trust, both of which are extremely important in the sales process.

Moreover, the 'ethos' or 'purpose' enables a salesperson to transcend simply selling 'what' their company offers. Instead, they communicate at a higher level, being able to connect with a prospect on a meeting of values. Having a sales conversation on this basis is always likely to be more effective as there is a recognition of mutual understanding underlying any communication that takes place.

If a customer feels understood, they are much more likely to be open to the suggestions a salesperson makes. When a customer feels their beliefs and those of the salesperson are aligned, it will make them more comfortable that any offering will meet their requirements. This mutual understanding leads to the salesperson being more trusted and credible with the customer, who will feel they see the world in the same way.

Of course, at some point in the buying journey the client will want to know more of the details of the acquisition. However, by this time, and with a meeting of values, they may very well be predisposed to buying. With emotion playing such a big role in decision making, a customer who believes they are understood by, and aligned with, a salesperson is more likely to resolve to make the purchase.

This becomes a very different conversation than salespeople trying to convince prospects using the minutiae of product or service details as selling points. This is often where sales becomes adversarial, with prospects 'objecting' as to whether particular aspects of a proposition are indeed worthwhile or not. The most effective salespeople today often don't even need to have many of those conversations. Once the customer has already made their mind up to purchase, the details can often be worked out in an atmosphere where both parties want the acquisition to take place.

2. The core deliverable or value proposition

As Albert Einstein said, 'If you can't explain it simply, you don't understand it well enough'.[13]

There are too many organizations that fail to truly understand the nature of the value that they provide to customers. Salespeople can often explain the value if given five minutes, but struggle to encompass it in a single phrase. However, in a world where there is so much noise, and obtaining the attention of prospects and customers is increasingly difficult, it is important to be able to express the core deliverable of a business in a few simple words.

Salespeople and marketing teams are now required to use media channels such as blogs and social platforms, etc., in order to engage with prospects and customers. Like all media channels these platforms demand good content in order to be effective, and so sales and marketing departments need to provide valuable material to enable them to engage with their customers. This content has to relate in some way to the core offering of the business. This is to ensure that, somewhere down the line, the attention and continued engagement of prospects and customers leads to purchases.

In terms of a business guaranteeing its communications are consistent, part of delivering a cohesive tone of voice is ensuring that everyone in the organization has a clinical understanding of the value it delivers to customers. It is necessary to be able to articulate the value proposition in a single phrase or sentence. Of course, when required, salespeople can expand upon the value for a prospect.

Unless people within an organization have an acute understanding of their value proposition for customers, it becomes almost impossible to create content of value around that core proposition. This can lead to content being produced that is of little worth to a prospect. Indeed, it is commonplace to see content online that does not resonate in any way, even when you are a target purchaser of the business concerned.

Alternatively, valuable material may be created, but the content is ineffective in taking customers down a purchase journey. Ultimately, for the sales and marketing to be useful, two objectives must be fulfilled. First, the prospect or customer has to receive value in order for them to continue to give their attention to the material. Second, over time, the content has to be able to generate an appetite for the company's products or services. The buying journey can be of varied length and in certain circumstances can be quite long, but if the content never leads prospects or customers to make purchases then it is completely inadequate.

For example, a recruitment agent might define its value proposition as 'obtaining the right talent for your business'. As part of its content offering it may produce material on topics such as 'how to identify the available talent in any market place', 'how to read between the lines of a CV', '10 top tips for effective interviews', and 'getting the cultural fit right – how to match candidates and companies successfully'.

In the appropriate circumstances, this material will have a value for prospects and customers. Of course, some people will take the content and attempt to undertake the process themselves. This is fine, as no company will turn every engaged prospect into a customer. See the Digital Sales Funnel in Chapter 4.

However, there will be individuals who, on reading how involved the process is, from identifying the correct talent to reading CVs properly and getting the right cultural fit, will decide to seek the assistance of a recruitment firm. In this way, as well as providing insights and value for customers, in some circumstances, the content will create an appetite for the recruitment company's services.

Moreover, by creating material of genuine value the recruitment firm would have earned some credibility and trust with potential purchasers. If the content delivers real insight to a buyer then there is also a good chance it will have some influence on their criteria of purchase, and so a customer's expectations may already be a good fit for the recruitment company's offering. After all, it is the recruitment company's material that has already had an impact on the buyer's views.

Therefore, much of the content produced has to ultimately relate, in some way, to the core proposition of the business. Without a clear and clinical understanding of what this is, it will not be possible for sales or marketing people to utilize the channels at their disposal effectively.

One way for sales and marketing departments to identify their core value proposition is to go through the following process.

First, a list must be made of all the products and services the company supplies. Then, against that inventory, each target customer group must be put alongside the different offerings for which they are a potential purchaser. For each customer group and offering, a list of the challenges a prospect may have that could lead them to the purchase of the particular product or service, needs to be made.

Having these challenges doesn't necessarily mean people will be beating a path to your door. They may find a competitor. There will also be alternative solutions to the same predicaments. For example, needing to find a new member of staff could lead me to our recruitment agent mentioned previously. Alternatively, I could decide to advertise in a local paper or search appropriate online platforms for potential candidates. In other words, there are a number of potential solutions to the problem.

When listing these challenges, you are looking for the big core issues, rather than the minutiae of details. In this way, for any one product or service, and customer base, it is unlikely you will have more than five or six points at most. On the other hand, you should not settle for less than three. Ultimately, this exercise allows you to identify the core motivations as to why someone would buy your products or services. Of course there are exceptions, but to not even be able to come up with three reasons would lead to a concern as to the commercial viability of the offering.

In order to ensure that you only focus on the core challenges of the customer, it can be helpful to think in terms of cause and effect. In this exercise we are trying to capture the root causes, rather than the multitude of effects. For example, I worked with a management training business. Its customers were mainly HR directors at medium to large organizations. In this case, there was one product and one customer base.

When we started listing the prospect's challenges the managing director wrote down, 'We can't find the right training provider'. This could indeed be a problem, but I suggested instead that it was an effect. The real question was, 'Why were they looking for training in the first place?' The managing director then suggested the potential customer may have a skills gap in the organization; they may have a high staff attrition rate or low staff morale. These are causes. It is not always easy, however, to distinguish between a cause and an effect, and it may take some time to decipher between the two.

Below are a couple of working examples to provide you with more of an idea of how this functions.

Finance Directors Ltd has one offering, which is to provide organizations with part-time finance directors. It has one client base: owner/managers of companies with 10–60 employees that have a turnover of £3–15 million. With only one client base and one offering, only a single set of challenges needs to be produced. Ultimately, what we are asking is, 'What are the key issues your company solves?' We identified these as:

- I am struggling to make good decisions without more of an understanding of my finances.

- I can't secure the lending I require and I am not sure why.

- Without certain financial information at my disposal, my business is not saleable.

- Without particular financial knowledge it is difficult to get the business strategy right.

With the challenges listed, the way to identify the value proposition is to try to capture the essence of all the issues into one sentence. Obviously, you won't necessarily get all the nuances, but the crux of the issues should be summarized in one phrase. In other words, having listed the challenges, the question you are asking is, 'Ultimately, what does this mean?'

For Finance Directors Ltd we defined the value proposition as, 'Using financial expertise to unlock business profit'.

All of these challenges exist because of a lack of financial know-how. Whether it is making good decisions, securing lending, selling a business or getting the right strategy in place, all of these are to achieve greater success, and in commercial organizations, that means profit. The value proposition summarizes the essence of all the challenges identified.

The London Insurance Company is an insurance broker supplying two client bases. The first is high-net-worth individuals in London. The second is London businesses turning over between £3–50 million with 10–250 staff. In this scenario, two sets of challenges need to be identified for the two different client bases.

For the high-net-worth individuals, the following issues were determined:

- I have insurance requirements that fall outside of the mainstream (eg, large wine or art collections).

- I don't have the time or patience for this.

- I am concerned that if I have a claim I will not get paid out.

For the businesses the challenges were as follows:

- I am worried that I don't really understand all my exposures and liabilities.

- I don't have time.

- I am concerned as to whether, if I have a claim, I will get paid.

- I have certain areas of compliance to which I must adhere.

What is interesting about listing the customers' challenges, is that there is almost always overlap between the different offerings and customer groups. Therefore, even when a business seems to supply a very complex array of products or services, it is normally possible to have a cohesive value proposition by looking at the business from the customer's viewpoint.

Although the London Insurance Company has two different client bases, one business and one consumer, there are still plenty of similarities in their challenges. While the high-net-worth customers may have requirements that fall outside of mainstream insurance, businesses are also concerned about their own exposures and liabilities. Both sets of groups are time poor and, because of the amounts of money involved, are concerned to ensure that in the event of a claim, they will be paid out.

Although on the face of it there seem to be seven separate issues between the two sets of challenges, the reality is that with the overlap, there are more like four completely separate points. By getting to the heart of these we can then create the value proposition, which for the London Insurance Company was identified as, 'guaranteed protection'.

From having unusual insurance requirements to understanding all exposures and liabilities, the point is that people want to know they are protected. Similarly, even when they don't have the time to examine all the details, customers want the reassurance that in the event of a claim, they will be paid.

Salespeople and marketing departments must ensure they have a clinical understanding of their value proposition. Of course, for salespeople, this allows them to articulate the offering when in a face-to-face scenario. It also brings with it a perception of what really matters to customers, and the aspects of the products or services that are likely to be of less importance.

Similarly, when utilizing online platforms, it will not be possible to create relevant content of value without understanding the core proposition of the business. Moreover, in terms of tone of voice, when you combine the purpose of the organization, together with the value proposition, it starts to become easier to brief all members of staff to ensure mistakes in communication do not occur.

In order to demonstrate, let's revisit our college. This further educational establishment has one offering, which is a variety of vocational courses. However, it has two sets of customers. Set one is the students who take the courses. Set two is the local employers who use the college for their own staff, and without whom the college couldn't secure the success rate of students going directly into work.

First, we list the challenges facing the students, for which the college is a possible solution:

- What are my career choices? What am I going to do next?
- Where will I fit in (sense of belonging, what others will think of me, peer group pressure)?
- Will I be able to achieve the things I want (aspirations)?

Second, we list the challenges facing the employers:

- How does the business cost-effectively keep staff up to date with new legislation and compliance requirements?
- How do we stay competitive?
- How do we recruit in the most cost effective way possible?
- Reputation (looking after our own reputation in the market with aspects such as corporate social responsibility).

In essence we drilled these seven issues into four core challenges:

- Career choices – will I be able to achieve the things I want to do? Today's career choices are obviously inextricably linked to fulfilling future aspirations.
- Where will I fit in? Having a sense of belonging is a basic human need. People need to fit in with friends, peer group and other influencers such as parents.
- Competitiveness – in order to compete, businesses have to train their staff in the latest compliance and regulations. Training and personal development can also be a way of achieving competitive advantage over rivals. Meanwhile, apprenticeships and other schemes can be a way for companies to recruit in the most cost-effective way in order to stay competitive.
- Reputation – students care what others, such as their friends and peer group, think. Companies worry about their own reputation in the market place.

These four core challenges were then summarized into one value proposition, which encompassed the essence of these issues: 'commercial achievement'. Whether it is being delivered for students or employers the core deliverable of the college is to enable 'commercial achievement'.

We now understand that the purpose of the college is that it believes in 'a return on education'. Its value proposition is to enable 'commercial achievement'. Using these two criteria alone, it starts to become possible to see how an organization can ensure that all communications across the business are cohesive. Meanwhile, salespeople and marketers alike gain a focus, and have an innate understanding of what is being delivered to customers in two simple sentences.

However, there is one more aspect required in order to ensure the 'tone of voice' of the company is clearly defined.

3. The emotional selling proposition

The story is famously told of IBM salespeople in the '70s, faced with increasing competition, using the phrase, 'no one ever got fired for buying IBM'.[14] This was a purely emotional message based on the fear of making a wrong decision. Yet in an environment where a purchaser's reputation and credibility were on the line, it was an extremely powerful point. Even now, many salespeople, marketers and organizations still fail to determine their emotional selling proposition.

As the professor of neuroscience, Antonio Damasio stated, 'We are not thinking machines that feel. We are feeling machines that think'.[15] Emotion plays a huge part in the decisions that we make. If we know this is the case, then why would marketers and salespeople leave emotion to chance? If our purchasing decisions are severely affected by our feelings, wouldn't it make sense for an organization to define what it is selling emotionally?

There are lots of different ways of describing the same product or service. Certain language will conjure up particular feelings. Specific images will also invoke distinct emotions. Therefore, marketers and salespeople have to define their emotional proposition. In other words, how do you want people to feel when they experience your offering? What does your core deliverable mean emotionally for customers?

Without defining their emotional proposition, businesses will be leaving it to chance. This could damage an organization. If the emotions that a customer feels are incongruent with the business proposition, then the organization will not be trusted. The customer will not necessarily be able to articulate 'why', but it won't 'feel' right. So, for example, an enterprise that sells candles might decide its emotional selling proposition is 'romance'. In this scenario, the company logo could not be black, as we do not associate that colour with love, passion or relationships. If a company were to make this mistake, the whole proposition may not resonate well with customers. Ultimately, the conflicting communications will make it less likely that a customer buys.

It is improbable that a business will deliver a cohesive experience across the organization without defining its emotional selling proposition. From the language and images used on the website, to any content created for social media, it is quite likely that there will be a disconnect between all these channels. The tone of e-mails, how the phone is answered, the clothes that are worn to meetings – all should be influenced by the emotional selling proposition. Without this being properly prescribed by the organization, it is unlikely that a company will get it right.

The emotional selling proposition is not something that should necessarily be articulated outside of an organization. It is an internal benchmark. Like the compass that always points north, the emotional selling proposition ensures that there is a consistency in a company's communications. Rather than explicitly telling customers what the emotional selling proposition is, it is often more powerful as an aspect of the experience that customers just feel. They may not use exactly the same words as used by a business internally, but the general sentiment conveyed by the customers would be true.

For example, Nike is named after the goddess of victory in Greek mythology. Emotionally, the brand stands for 'winning'.[16] Everything it does is about performance and being the best you can be.[17] If this was explicitly stated it would probably spoil the magic. The emotional proposition would be so overt that it may go from being aspirational to almost being pretentious or arrogant.

The power of this emotional proposition is that it is implied. By not being explicitly stated, there is an association with being a 'winner' when one wears Nike, without it becoming pompous or seemingly egotistical.

Even when brands do state their emotional selling proposition, it is not constantly 'in your face'. Harley Davidson emotionally sells 'freedom'.[18] While it has used this word in certain communications and campaigns, most of the time it is implied.[19] It is not constantly used in all its publicity. Again, if it was overused the danger is it might lose some of its resonance. Implying a feeling can often be more powerful than explicitly stating a position.

Let's go back to our college. We had already defined the purpose of the college as believing in 'a return on education'. The value proposition is to enable 'commercial achievement' for students and employers alike. With regard to the emotional selling proposition, two questions had to be asked. How do we want people to feel when they experience the college? What does the core deliverable of 'commercial achievement' mean emotionally for customers?

Of course, two separate vocational colleges could have defined their purpose, value proposition and emotional selling proposition quite differently. This being the case they could both offer the same courses and yet be poles apart in the experience students receive. In many ways, this is exactly the point, as there is room in almost all market places for an array of suppliers.

When the college began thinking about its emotional selling proposition it originally started to use words such as hope, optimism and aspiration. Of course, these emotions would seem to be appropriate for an establishment where people go to learn and improve themselves. However, these sentiments did not seem to quite fit.

The value proposition of the college is to deliver 'commercial achievement'. If as a student you study to be a car mechanic or plumber, you don't 'hope' to get a job at the end. There is little point in studying unless you have some degree of assurance that the likelihood is you will find work. Similarly, as an employer, if you take on an apprentice, you don't want to 'hope' it works out. Rather, you would like to think that at the end of the process you will have a good employee.

So we defined the emotional selling proposition as 'certainty'. In this crazy, changeable world in which we live, the college provides some degree of assurance that, by investing your time in one of its courses, you will come out with a career. Bearing in mind 94 per cent of students go straight into work, with others securing work after a little while, this is a valid position to take. Similarly, employers can be confident that by investing time in an apprentice, they will have a well-trained employee at the end of the process.

If the college had decided its emotional selling proposition was 'hope', the language it used would have been quite different to defining its emotional selling proposition as 'certainty'. With this emotional proposition, the language is necessarily bold and confident, and the outcomes suggested have a hint of inevitability about them.

With so many different individuals within an organization potentially communicating on a multitude of channels, it is vital that guidance is given to employees to ensure the company presents itself in a cohesive way at all times. Mission statements can often be misinterpreted, as they are frequently generic and extremely aspirational. Throwing lots of guidelines at individuals is normally unhelpful as they are often not read or remembered. Yet businesses are concerned, in an era where everyone has the potential to communicate, about how to safeguard their reputation.

By defining the purpose of the business, its core deliverable to customers and its emotional selling proposition, an extremely tight brief can be given to all stakeholders. It is easy to remember and less likely to be misinterpreted.

The college wanted to encourage all administrative staff, teachers and other stakeholders to communicate on social platforms. The brief was simple:

We believe in 'a return on education'.

We enable employers and students to obtain 'commercial achievement'.

Emotionally we deliver 'certainty'.

In terms of defining a tone of voice for an organization, this is a tight brief that is memorable and understandable.

The same definitions can be used by marketing to ensure all its communications are consistent. Of course, this type of understanding is also vital for salespeople who want to 'win' business for a company. Whether it is generating leads online, or in face-to-face meetings with prospects, it is imperative that salespeople have a clear idea of what an organization delivers and stands for, in order to be able to undertake their sales role successfully.

Endnotes

1 Google Docs: Paul Sawers (2011) Google Docs: A potted history, *TheNextWeb.com,* published 2 September [online] http://thenextweb. com/google/2011/09/02/15-tips-to-get-the-most-out-of-google-docs/ [accessed 24 December 2015]

'*Google Docs was released to Google Apps users in February 2007, presentations were added into the mix in September that year and then Google Docs, alongside other Google Apps, left beta mode in July 2009.*'

2 SkyDrive: Richard MacManus (2007) Windows Live SkyDrive launched – enters a crowded online storage, *ReadWrite.com,* published 9 August [online] http://readwrite.com/2007/08/09/windows_live_ skydrive_launched_online_storage [accessed 24 December 2015]

'*Today Microsoft announced Windows Live SkyDrive, the final product name for its online storage solution – previously known as Windows Live Folders. Windows Live SkyDrive has a few new features and enhanced UI, in line with upcoming changes across other Windows Live services.*'

3 Dropbox: (undated) Company background, Dropbox.com [online] https:// www.dropbox.com/news/company-info [accessed 24 December 2015]

'*Founded: June 2007 by Drew Houston and Arash Ferdowsi. Launched: September 2008 as a simple way to bring your files anywhere and share them easily.*'

4 Amazon Cloud Drive: (2011) Press release, *Amazon,* published 29 March [online] http://phx.corporate-ir.net/phoenix.zhtml?ID=1543596&c= 176060&p=irol-newsArticle [accessed 24 December 2015]

'*SEATTLE, Mar 29, 2011 (BUSINESS WIRE) – Amazon.com, Inc. (NASDAQ:AMZN) today announced the launch of Amazon Cloud Drive (www.amazon.com/clouddrive)... Cloud Drive allows customers to upload and store all kinds of digital files; music, photos, videos and documents can be stored securely and are available via web browser on any computer.*'

5 Apple iCloud: Apple Press Info. (2011) Apple Introduces iCloud. *Apple.* Published 6 June [online] https://www.apple.com/pr/library/2011/06/06 Apple-Introduces-iCloud.html [accessed 24 December 2015]

'*Apple® today introduced iCloud®, a breakthrough set of free new cloud services that work seamlessly with applications on your iPhone®, iPad®, iPod touch®, Mac® or PC to automatically and wirelessly store your content in iCloud and automatically and wirelessly push it to all your devices.*'

6 Cloud computing: Zoe Diamadi, Abhijit Dubey, Darren Pleasance and Ashish Vora (2011) Winning in the SMB Cloud: charting a path to success, *McKinsey & Company,* published July [online] http://www.mckinsey.com/client_service/high_tech/latest_thinking/winning_in_the_smb_cloud [accessed 24 December 2015]

'Virtually all of the largest technology players... are making significant cloud investments as are a number of smaller and newer entrants... and it quickly becomes clear that the cloud landscape is not only increasingly crowded, but will certainly be evolving as key players jockey for position in the coming years.'

7 Innocent: (2014) Breaking news: fruit is good for you, innocent, published 26 June [online] http://www.innocentdrinks.co.uk/blog/2014/june/breaking-news-fruit-is-good-for-you [accessed 24 December 2015]

'innocent was started with the aim of making it easier for people to do themselves some good. Our purpose as a company is to make natural, delicious food and drink that helps people live well and die old. Health is a priority for everyone, and it's extremely important to us.'

8 Innocent mechanism: (undated) Our purpose, *Innocent* [online] http://www.innocentdrinks.co.uk/us/careers [accessed 24 December 2015]

'... Everything innocent makes will always be 100% natural, delicious and nutritionally net-positive, so people are physically and mentally better off after they have had our drinks than before.'

9 Persuasion: Jared Lewis, Demand Media (undated) Repetition as a persuasive strategy, *Houston Chronicle* [online] http://smallbusiness.chron.com/repetition-persuasive-strategy-26001.html [accessed 24 December 2015]

Jared Lewis refers to psychological studies undertaken by J.T. Cachiappo and Richard Petty, who were innovators in this area of research in the late 1970s and 1980s. Jared writes: *'They concluded that low to moderate levels of repetition within a message tend to create greater agreement with the message, along with greater recall.'*

10 Bill Gates: Claudine Beaumont (2008) Bill Gates's dream: A computer in every home, *Telegraph,* published 27 June [online] http://www.telegraph.co.uk/technology/3357701/Bill-Gatess-dream-A-computer-in-every-home.html [accessed 24 December 2015]

'"When Paul Allen and I started Microsoft over 30 years ago, we had big dreams about software," recalls Gates. "We had dreams about the impact it could have. We talked about a computer on every desk and in every home."'

11 Mark Zuckerberg: (2012) United States Securities and Exchange Commission Washington, D.C. 20549 Form S-1 Registration Statement Under the Securities Act of 1933 Facebook, Inc. sec.gov., published 1 February [online] http://www.sec.gov/Archives/edgar/data/1326801/000119312512034517/d287954ds1.htm#toc287954_10 [accessed 24 December 2015]

'Letter from Mark Zuckerberg: Facebook was not originally created to be a company. It was built to accomplish a social mission – to make the world more open and connected.'

12 Ken Blanchard: (undated) Our Story, *The Ken Blanchard Companies* [online] https://www.kenblanchard.com/About-Us/Our-Story [accessed 24 December 2015]

'Drs. Ken and Marjorie Blanchard incorporated The Ken Blanchard Companies in 1979 with three simple goals – to make a difference in people's lives, to drive human worth and effectiveness in the workplace, and to help each organization we work with become the provider, employer, and investment of choice.'

13 Albert Einstein: (undated) Albert Einstein quotes, *Brainyquote* [online] http://www.brainyquote.com/quotes/quotes/a/alberteins383803.html [accessed 24 December 2015].

'If you can't explain it simply, you don't understand it well enough… Biography: Author Profession: Nationality: German. Born: March 14, 1879. Died: April 18, 1955.'

14 IBM: David Norris* (2014) What does the phrase 'Nobody ever got fired for choosing IBM' mean? Quora.com, published 29 April [online] https://www.quora.com/What-does-the-phrase-Nobody-ever-got-fired-for-choosing-IBM-mean [accessed 24 December]

*(David Norris, Diploma in Company Direction from The Institute of Directors • Upvoted by Rupert Baines, founded several start-ups, exec at several more, mentored many more. Two successful exits. • Marc Bodnick, Co-Founder, Elevation Partners)

'… if anything fails, it's YOUR FAULT. You made the wrong call… In many ways it's the perfect marketing message. The one thing every CIO wants to avoid is failure. Here IBM are saying, "choose us, your reputation will remain intact and you will be able to sleep at night".'

15 Antonio Damasio (1995) *Descartes' Error: Emotion, reason and the human brain*, First Avon Books, New York

'We are not thinking machines that feel. We are feeling machines that think.'

16 Nike: The Editors of Encyclopædia Britannica (undated) Nike, Greek goddess, *Encyclopedia Britannica* [online] http://www.britannica.com/topic/Nike-Greek-goddess [accessed 24 December 2015]

'Nike, in Greek religion, the goddess of victory, daughter of the giant Pallas and of the infernal River Styx... Nike is frequently hovering with outspread wings over the victor in a competition... Indeed, Nike gradually came to be recognized as a sort of mediator of success between gods and men.'

17 Nike marketing: Geraldine E. Willigan (1992) High-performance marketing: an interview with Nike's Phil Knight, *Harvard Business Review*, published July–August [online] https://hbr.org/1992/07/high-performance-marketing-an-interview-with-nikes-phil-knight [accessed 24 December 2015]

'Our advertising tries to link consumers to the Nike brand through the emotions of sports and fitness. We show competition, determination, achievement, fun, and even the spiritual rewards of participating in those activities.'

18 Harley – freedom: Brad VanAuken, The Blake Project (2014) Linking brands and positive emotions, *Branding Strategy Insider*, published 29 July [online] http://www.brandingstrategyinsider.com/2014/01/linking-brands-and-positive-emotions.html#.Vnvc6vHQ_3w [accessed 24 December 2015]

'Sometimes brands can help people feel certain emotions, emotions that may even be only tangentially related to the products themselves. Brands can create tremendous appeal by linking to or promising desired emotions... Harley Davidson promises freedom of the road along with the comradeship of kindred spirits.'

19 Freedom – implied: Glenn Rifkin (1997) How Harley Davidson revs its brand, *Strategy + Business* (originally published by Booz & Company) published 1 October [online] http://www.strategy-business.com/article/12878?gko=ffaa3 [accessed 24 December 2015]

'As an American icon, Harley has come to symbolize freedom, rugged individualism, excitement and a sense of "bad boy rebellion". "Harley reflects many things Americans dream about", said Benson P. Shapiro, a consultant and a marketing professor at the Harvard Business School.'

The lead generation model in a digital world

04

The essence of AIDA is as follows:[1]

Awareness – the first step in the sales process is to ensure prospects are 'aware' of your offering.

Interest – once the prospect is cognizant, the next stage is to get them interested in your product or service.

Desire – the prospect moves from being curious to actually wanting the offer.

Action – tangible steps are taken to move towards the purchase and make the acquisition.

AIDA captures the emotions of a purchase journey exceptionally well. The buying cycle can be extremely short, for example, obtaining some chocolate in a supermarket. Alternatively, it can be very long, as in a company investing in a major software platform at a huge cost of both time and money; the basic process is the same. What changes, of course, is the speed at which the buyer moves from each state. In every purchase journey the prospect has to be aware of the offering, show interest in it, decide they want to buy and then take action to make it happen.

However, it is when AIDA, a good conceptual reference for the different states through which a buyer goes, is combined with the traditional sales funnel that it is no longer an appropriate model in today's business environment. The basic concept of how the sales funnel works has not altered much since it was joined with AIDA in the 1920s.[2] It really is quite startling that when the world has changed in so many fundamental ways, most businesses are still utilizing a version of a standard that was first conceptualized at the end of the 19th century.

The sales, marketing or purchase funnel is most commonly associated with Elias St. Elmo Lewis from an article he wrote in 1898.[3] Since then it has been referred to by a variety of names and can be seen in many iterations. In 1924, in his book *Bond Salesmanship*, William W. Townsend combined the sales funnel with AIDA.[4] This acronym was created by C.P Russell in an article in the trade magazine *Printers' Ink* in 1921,[5] but it should be noted that as early as 1893 many of the concepts that evolved into AIDA were already being written about.[6] In fact, an almost identical formula was codified by Frank Hutchinson Dukesmith in volume two of the magazine *Salesmanship* in 1904.[7]

Imagine undertaking disciplines such as human resources, operational management or leadership and relying on practices from well over 100 years ago. Yet, that is exactly the situation throughout the world of sales and marketing. It almost defies logic that this could possibly be the best approach today.

There have been a multitude of variations of this sales funnel over the years. Although there are nuances that change, and at times different language has been introduced, ultimately the general principles established by William Townsend's joining of AIDA with the sales funnel have, in essence, remained unaltered. Therefore, to remind us of how this funnel worked, and why it needs to change, we will rely on this basic model as seen below.

Figure 4.1 Traditional AIDA

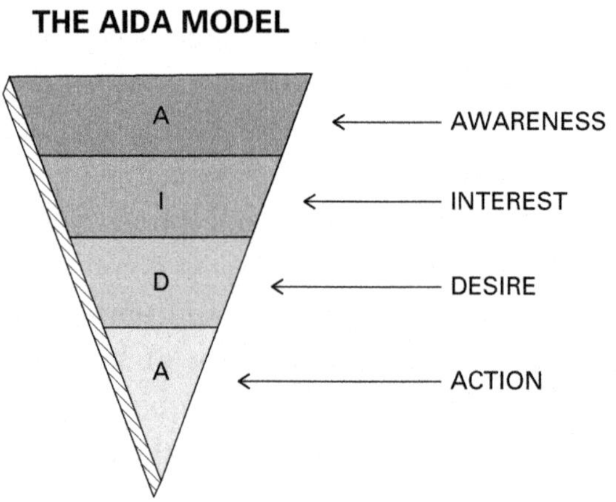

THE AIDA MODEL

Obtaining awareness, in sales and marketing terms, was a pure numbers game. Whether marketers were sending out a direct mail, advertising in a trade magazine or creating commercials for television, the idea was to try to reach the biggest relevant audience possible. So, for example, if a marketing department wanted to reach high net worth individuals to promote a luxury car, they may have discriminated by postcode, only mailing their literature to more affluent parts of the country.

Similarly, in their role, salespeople would traditionally knock on as many doors as possible, either by literally walking the streets or by utilizing the phone. They would dial hundreds of numbers, of individuals that had been identified as target prospects for whatever products or services they were selling.

The reason for wanting to reach huge volumes was that, at any particular time, most people would not be attentive to the communications. Therefore, in order to get enough people into the interest part of the funnel, large numbers of prospects had to be targeted at the top.

Of course, with many consumer offerings, marketing departments could be responsible for taking a customer from the top of the funnel to the bottom. So, in areas such as fast-moving consumer goods, for example a soft drink product, the marketing team may be charged with creating awareness, interest and desire through media such as television, radio and print. While some of this material could even elicit action, this was also generated with good product placement and point-of-sale literature within the stores.

Other sections of the consumer market employed salespeople. So, for example, a central marketing team may be responsible for creating awareness and interest throughout the country for a particular make of vehicle. It would then be left to the salespeople in respective showrooms to generate desire and action. Of course, provincial dealerships may also undertake localized marketing campaigns to gain awareness.

In business-to-business environments, one of the roles of marketing would be to create awareness. This would often assist salespeople who, when engaging customers, may already have some credibility, in as much as the prospect knew of the company they were representing.

Marketing departments would also run campaigns to create an amount of interest and, in some cases, desire. Leads passed on to salespeople might be prospects that had shown some interest, in other words responded to a call to action from an advert or mailer. Meanwhile, 'hot leads' as they were often called, might be prospects who had shown a real desire for the offer. It was then left to salespeople to turn interest into desire and desire into a sale.

Fundamentally, the traditional sales funnel relied on sales and marketing functions paying to obtain awareness. This was achieved by interrupting a prospect when they were busy with another activity. So, marketers would remunerate media organizations in order to be able to interrupt their target audience when these viewers, listeners and readers were engaged with the programmes and other content that had been created. Similarly, salespeople would call on individuals during working hours when they knew customers would be in their office and at their desks.

Today, there is an organizational challenge in that fewer people are at their desks and answering their phones.[8] This is due to developments such as flexible and home working. This is combined with technological advances such as number recognition, voicemails and the ubiquitous use of e-mail, text messaging and messaging apps such as Facebook Messenger and WhatsApp.[9] However, logistics apart, there is another fundamental challenge with simply interrupting people to gain awareness.

In a world where we had little access to information and choice, people would pay attention, to a degree, to the interruptions they received. This is because they would often provide individuals with some value. So, for example, a couple looking to buy a property, and thinking about mortgages, might very well give a mortgage proposition, received by direct mail, some consideration. A company's marketing would often be a resource used by consumers in a world where information was relatively scarce.

Similarly, a CEO exploring some management training options might have engaged with a salesperson who called them cold in order to tell them about the management training programmes that their company offers. Again, in a world where gathering information and sourcing suppliers was not always easy, the CEO, despite having their day interrupted, may have found the phone call valuable.

The problem for companies still trying to buy awareness at the top of the funnel is simple: fewer people are paying attention.[10] The marketing interruptions via television, radio, magazine adverts and direct mail etc., are often deemed to provide little or no value for consumers.[11] This is in a commercial climate where individuals can access almost all the information they require 24/7, at their convenience. Purchase journeys were often reactive, with prospects responding to a company's literature and offers. Today, people are inclined to be proactive, searching online and accessing their networks when looking for particular products, services and solutions.[12]

This is even more stark for salespeople who are often challenged with generating their own sales leads. People are less inclined to respond favourably to what are seen as quite invasive techniques such as knocking on doors, making cold calls or sending unsolicited e-mails, texts or messages on social platforms such as LinkedIn.[13]

There are two major reasons for this situation. First, consumers have now been empowered, with access to information whenever it is required. This diminishes any value that previously existed in the visits and calls that prospects used to receive. Therefore, interrupting people in a particularly disruptive way is looked upon, in the main, as extremely irritating and an act of pure self-interest. In other words, salespeople are looking to peddle their wares, with nothing in it for the prospect. This is because customers are confident that if, and when, they are in the market for whatever is being sold, they will be able to access the information themselves. Consequently, their mindset is that, if they need to, they will call the salesperson rather than the other way round. It is a classic case of 'don't call us, we'll call you'.

Second, we live in a world where we are bombarded with information 24/7. We are constantly connected, receiving a plethora of communications via telephone calls, texts, messaging services, e-mails, social media platforms and alerts and notifications from apps and other devices. It is difficult to cope with the seemingly infinite amount of material we receive. Therefore, we are increasingly personalizing everything in order to be able to manage.

We can download news, music and magazines, creating individual edited versions just to suit us. We can construct television schedules that fit in with our timetables using digital platforms and catch-up services. Finally, we can discriminate between calls and messages, prioritizing some, directing others to specific folders, and assigning individual ringtones for different people.

In this environment, when a salesperson simply cuts through all our filters with a phone call, text or e-mail, we often feel violated. Certainly, there is a sense of being held with complete disregard. This is not the best way for a salesperson to approach a prospect with a view to initiating a purchase.

Today, many salespeople are attempting to utilize social media while relying on the traditional sales funnel as their overall model. In the same way as they would previously have made cold calls or sent unsolicited e-mails, many are now making the equivalent uninvited approaches within these social platforms.

Digital selling is not about using social media for volume prospecting in order to find enough 'interested' people to take them further down the traditional sales funnel. Within social platforms, this behaviour will most likely come across as extremely forceful. Consequently, it is unlikely to be received favourably.

Despite this, 'lead scraping', as it is commonly known, is being undertaken. It involves extracting information from social platforms and the web, and using it to create a pool of prospects. It is a direct result of salespeople still trying to play the numbers game at the top of the funnel. With the telephone and other channels proving less effective than they once were, and with their customers spending an ever-increasing amount of time online,[14] salespeople are trying to make the traditional funnel work in a digital environment. This is essentially the old adage of trying to 'put a square peg in a round hole'.

Lead scraping works in a variety of ways. First, demographic information can be scraped and used to compile lists of prospects. So, for example, a platform such as LinkedIn can be mined to search for people with particular job titles, in specific industries and locations, and in companies of a certain size. Similarly, social media monitoring and web-scraping software can be used to identify prospects and extract contact information, using keywords and scraping data from sites such as business directories. They can be applied to identify when certain keywords are being used within conversations, which salespeople can then scan. Salespeople can also join groups, forums and networks to listen in on the dialogue. If a salesperson catches the slightest hint that an individual might be in the market for, or would be able to use, their products or services, they will make a direct approach.

Monitoring conversations in order to contribute with valuable comments, via insights or recommendations, is legitimate, but simply listening to these discussions as a way of building volume for prospecting the old fashioned way is not good practice.

Cold sales messages sent to individuals within platforms such as LinkedIn or via other mechanisms such as text or e-mail are not seen any more favourably than the cold calls most people object to receiving via the phone. In fact, within social media platforms this approach can be worse.

It is no coincidence that these platforms are referred to as 'social media'. The word media, as we have explored in previous chapters, is appropriate because these are communication channels that are built on content. They have the ability to reach as wide a range of people as other media such as radio, television, newspapers and magazines.

The word 'social' suggests some sort of companionship or connectedness. It is indeed the case that conversations often occur between individuals who already have some sort of relationship. Of course, you can meet a complete stranger at a 'social' gathering and become friendly. At a function, you can join in a conversation that is taking place, with remarks that add insight or value. This can also happen online. If your contribution at the function or online is deemed worthwhile by others, they are likely to welcome you into the discussion and engage more.

However, if at a 'social' gathering the first communication you had with an individual was that person trying to sell you something, even if it was based on a conversation they overheard earlier, you would probably find it presumptuous, intrusive and overly forceful. This is exactly how a salesperson will be perceived if they use listening mechanisms online to make sales approaches to people they do not know. Of course, while every so often they might 'get lucky', in the main, this approach will be ineffective. In fact, worse still, it is likely over the long term to have a damaging effect on the salesperson's reputation.

The other challenge in trying to use the conventional sales funnel in a digital environment, is that prospects no longer need the assistance of salespeople, or organizations, to go through the funnel. In traditional business-to-business selling, marketing teams may obtain awareness and even create some interest. Salespeople themselves would often initiate the awareness and interest through their own lead generation activities. Either way, with limited access to any other information, purchasers had little option other than to engage with salespeople in order to find out more.

For example, an advert in a trade magazine may have made an operations director aware of a piece of machinery. They became interested as they realized that it might enable them to streamline some of their internal procedures, potentially making them more profitable. Of course, a salesperson could initiate this awareness and interest themselves, through a cold call.

Either way, the next stage in the buying process would be to engage with potential suppliers of the equipment, and have some discussions with the relevant sales reps. There would be very few alternative options in order to pursue the purchase. Therefore, the salesperson would be invited in at the 'interest' stage of the funnel. In fact, sometimes a prospect might find out about a new product or service and feel that in their professional capacity, it was something they should know about. In this scenario, the salesperson may even have found themselves invited in at the awareness stage. Moreover, because customers were unable to take themselves through the purchase journey, with some diligent following up, the salesperson could keep track of where their prospect was in the buying cycle. Of course, the salesperson may have found themselves pitching against competitors, but it was still relatively easy to measure where along the buying process the prospect was at any given time.

This is simply no longer the case. In most situations, individuals can tap into a rich array of information, including product and service specifications, case studies, reviews, articles, videos, testimonials, opinions and social proof. Buyers can access their own networks, independent experts, forums, websites, blogs and other platforms where they deem credible knowledge and advice can be obtained.

Using the classic funnel model, there is now no reason for a prospect to engage a salesperson until much later in the buying process, if at all. Even in complex purchases, customers are often able to get as far as the desire part of the funnel before any salesperson needs to be involved. At this juncture, they will have most likely ascertained most, if not all of their requirements. This leaves the salesperson very little room to demonstrate value; they simply become service agents who are unable to influence the criteria of purchase and, therefore, which supplier, if any, wins the business. In addition, if the buyer cannot identify any real difference between suppliers, the salesperson is likely to be hit hard on price, which then becomes the one distinguishable differentiator.

In other words, with the changes the web and digital technology have brought, using the traditional sales funnel as a model makes it harder for salespeople to engage prospects at the attention and interest stages of the buying cycle. This is where they are most likely to be able to influence the criteria of purchase and, therefore, make an impact on their company's bottom line.

Buyers no longer need salespeople to go through the sales funnel. Therefore, even if a salesperson manages to engage an individual at the awareness or interest stage of the process, it is much harder for them to then track where their prospect is in the buying cycle at any given time. This is because purchasers may go off and undertake their own independent journey after an initial conversation with a salesperson. If a salesperson fails to earn credibility, elicit a degree of trust and add value during these early interactions, there is a greater chance of them losing the opportunity than when buyers had to rely on someone to guide them through the purchase, and couldn't do it for themselves.

The problem is that the traditional funnel has no mechanism for calculating value creation, provides no model for establishing credibility and does not measure engagement with the prospect. Instead, it focuses on volume. By interrupting enough people, the salesperson will have sufficient interested individuals to then create some desire in some, and achieve a certain level of sales. That is why the traditional model goes from a wide top, where the key is to reach as many people as possible, down to a small base, with prospects continually falling out of the process until relatively few buy. Quite simply, this model is no longer fit for purpose.

It is abundantly clear, therefore, that we need a fresh standard to reflect the realities of the 21st century. Below is that new model, the Digital Sales Funnel.

Figure 4.2 Digital Sales Funnel

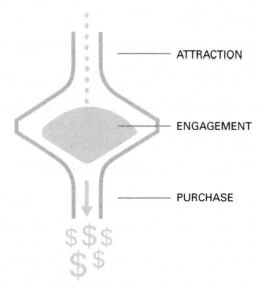

ATTRACTION

ENGAGEMENT

PURCHASE

Source: STICKYMARKETING.COM

As you can see, rather than the traditional cone shape, the new Digital Sales Funnel is more like an inverse hourglass.

The reason you now have a narrow top is that salespeople are no longer going to approach prospects using unwanted and invasive techniques, such as knocking door to door or cold calling. In today's business environment, salespeople are going to harness the potential of digital media in order to attract purchasers to them.

The wide top of the traditional cone was to reflect the volume activities of dialling hundreds of telephone numbers or sending out thousands of mailers. If prospects are now going to come to the salesperson, they are unlikely to flock hundreds or thousands at a time. Instead, there is more likely to be a steady drip feed of purchasers coming in ones, twos or a few at a time. Even if seasonality means that there are occasions when there are a greater number of approaches by buyers, the reality is that the mass volume activities are no longer necessary. Therefore, the top of the funnel is now much smaller.

The middle part of the funnel is now the widest component. This is in stark contrast to the cone where the funnel keeps narrowing. In the traditional model, this contraction reflects the reality that people would keep being screened out of the process until the salesperson was left to concentrate on a few prospects who had shown a real desire for their products or services. The salesperson would then focus on 'closing' some of these buyers in order to 'get the deal'.

So, a salesperson may start with a database of 500 companies. After cold calling the list, there may be 25 responsive individuals who agree to receive further information. The salesperson would then focus their activities on these 25 prospects, following up to see if they could create more interest or even some desire. This may result in five initial appointments. From this, three proposals may be sent. This may lead to more effort and meetings on the salesperson's part. Eventually, a deal may materialize.

The figures in this example are irrelevant, but the principle is sound. Whether it was a salesperson cold calling, or a marketing department sending out a direct mail to thousands, the point is that companies were choosing the target prospects. Individuals were not volunteering themselves. Consequently, most people were not going to be interested, and therefore would not respond positively.

If a marketing team sent out 5,000 mailers and received 10 responses, the marketing or sales team would then focus on the 10. This was because there was no cost-effective way of following up the other 4,990 to see if they received the mailer and whether they might be interested. What was a business going to do? Phone them all? Knock on each of their doors? Of course, theoretically, one could do so but no organization, in this scenario, would receive a return on investment from these activities.

Similarly, salespeople would concentrate on the interested individuals who came out of their initial calling. Of course, sales reps would revisit lists and data over time. However, after receiving a 'no' from a prospect it was not logical, or worthwhile, to go back to that person before there had been a significant time lapse.

It was also only worth a salesperson trying a company on a cold-calling list so many times before they gave up on ever speaking to the right person. This was because there were always people on a list to whom, and for whatever reason, the salesperson was never going to get to speak. Maybe they were not office based, refused to ever take cold calls or had an extremely protective gatekeeper. This being the case, if a salesperson didn't eventually give up on these particular prospects, they would end up with a calling list full of numbers of people they could never reach. Of course, this would be a list of diminishing returns.

The cone shape was, therefore, necessary. It reflected the reality that one would start out with a large prospect base, which would keep decreasing in numbers until a relatively tiny amount of actual purchasers emerged.

The Digital Sales Funnel works in a completely different way. First, it is no longer the salesperson or marketing department that intrusively chooses to communicate with an individual. Rather, in the new model, prospects determine to engage with them. They are, therefore, self-selecting.

This does not mean that every person who approaches a business is overflowing with uncontrollable enthusiasm to buy the company's products or services. They may be extremely passive at this juncture.

For example, an individual may have in mind that the lease on their current vehicle is ending in a year. As they are on holiday from work, they decide to take the opportunity to surf the web to see what sort of cars and deals are currently available. This may lead them onto a salesperson's review blog. Having found the articles extremely enlightening they are encouraged to sign up for monthly updates. At this point, while the prospect has entered the wide middle section of the new funnel, they are latent at this stage. Even if they decide to go ahead with a purchase, it is a year away.

The reason, however, that the middle section is wide, is that once someone has fallen into this part of the funnel, it is the salesperson's job to keep them there until they become a customer. In other words, there is no screening out as there is with the cone.

We inhabit a world today where the most precious resource, from a sales and marketing viewpoint, is attention. So once a prospect, however passive they may be, has voluntarily put their head above the parapet and chosen to engage with a salesperson or organization, they are too valuable an asset to be lost.

One of the main reasons for the cone-shaped funnel was that having contacted potentially thousands of prospects, a company had no cost-effective way of following all of them up. This is no longer the case. With customer relationship management software, e-mail marketing services and marketing automation systems, among other tools, individuals and companies can stay in contact with thousands of prospects for a relatively small cost. See Chapter 9 for more about technology to assist your digital selling efforts.

The fact that it is now possible to stay in contact and follow up vast numbers of individuals, and still deliver a return on investment, already makes the cone shape redundant. This is because it is no longer a commercial necessity to screen people out of the sales process in the way it was previously. Moreover, traditionally, it was the business that chose the prospects, and so there would be many people receiving direct mails or phone calls etc., for whom the offering was completely irrelevant. In the new model, it is the purchasers themselves who choose to approach the company. Therefore, because these individuals are self-selecting, there is even more reason to keep them in the funnel and not arbitrarily screen them out. However passive, the fact is that these people have shown themselves to have some interest in the organization.

Of course, although the aim of salespeople and marketing departments is to keep prospects in the middle of the funnel until they become customers, the reality is there will be erosion. Individuals will opt out of receiving information, may unsubscribe, or may simply ignore any communications; there is also a natural decline. In business-to-consumer marketing, individuals may die, move, or fall out of the target demographic as they get older or their circumstances change. Similarly, companies may change location, merge or go out of business. However, from the point of view of the salesperson, or marketing department, the idea is to prevent as much attrition as possible.

The traditional funnel was completely transactional in nature. Organizations would communicate messages, in volume, looking for a few prospects currently in the market to buy. They would then concentrate their efforts on turning some of this awareness and interest into purchases.

When looking for products and services today, the buying journey now starts with the customer going online and accessing their networks. With so much information available, the challenge is that salespeople end up involved in the process so late, if at all, that they have very little chance of influencing the criteria of purchase, which goes to the heart of successful selling.

Therefore, in order for salespeople to be able to influence the purchase criteria, they have to find a way of getting in front of customers earlier in the sales cycle. If much of the customer research takes place online,[15] that is the space where salespeople have to operate. If they can provide insight and information when the prospect is openly researching and looking for it, then they have a chance of influencing the person's thinking, whilst also building credibility and trust with that individual.

Social proof is also playing an increasingly vital role online. As the web goes social, and online platforms become one of the world's primary communication channels, it is easier for everyone to access the opinions and views of colleagues, family and friends. Therefore, the best marketers, lead generators and salespeople any organization has today are the 'engaged community' of individuals it builds around its business.

Word of mouth has always been the most powerful route to market for any company,[16] and today that is increasingly taking place online. From making actual referrals and recommendations to sharing videos and articles etc., it is the engaged community a company or salesperson builds around them that becomes increasingly responsible for generating awareness and interest in an organization's products or services.

This, in many ways, is the real opportunity. Although word of mouth has always been the most powerful channel to market, there was not historically that much a company could do in order to generate word-of-mouth recommendations. Of course, businesses would try to deliver the best products and services they could, with the hope that satisfied customers may tell others. In business-to-business environments, salespeople could ask those clients with whom they had a good relationship whether they knew of anyone else they could refer. In business-to-consumer marketing, companies would sometimes create 'recommend a friend' schemes, with rewards offered in order to encourage customers to tell others. Ultimately, though, considering just how powerful word of mouth is, there was not so much that could be done in order to obtain referrals.

Now, salespeople and marketing departments can elicit word of mouth and track its effectiveness. With everyone owning their own channels, people are often predisposed to sharing content that they deem worthwhile. Therefore, when companies and salespeople create content of value, not only will it engage existing customers and prospects, but it has the potential to be shared. It is this sharing that can be tracked and measured. Marketers and salespeople alike can then review the content. They can ascertain the material that is most effective and which is having the least impact. In so doing, they can continually try to refine and improve their output.

We are not talking about content going viral. This term refers to material 'spreading like a virus' across the web, and becoming an online sensation. In many business-to-business situations, where salespeople or marketing departments are communicating to niche audiences, this is unlikely to occur. Moreover, being seen by millions of people who could never buy your products or services won't necessarily improve the bottom line.

The real currency is 'social sharing', that is, material that engaged individuals within a salesperson's or company's community send to others. So, for example, a salesperson may have a weekly blog with 500 subscribers. Each week 25 people share the blog with one other person. In this way, the salesperson is generating awareness with 25 new people in the most credible way possible, via social proof. In this one small example our salesperson may reach over a thousand people during the year. These numbers would not be described as viral. Yet this 'social sharing' is extremely powerful.

This is why the middle of the funnel is the widest part. The more attention a salesperson or marketing team obtains, the more likely it is that their content is shared, their company is talked about and referrals are received. This, in turn, will attract others to the business who will then accrue inside the middle of the funnel. In other words, it is a virtuous circle.

In a world where everyone owns a channel, salespeople need to leverage the appropriate media in order to reach their prospects. In essence, this is undertaken by producing content of value. Content is the currency of media. It makes no difference whether it is a magazine, newspaper, radio station, TV station or any digital offering from websites and blogs to social media pages. It is the content that makes these platforms interesting.

As the French critic and journalist Jean-Baptiste Alphonse Karr once quipped, 'the more things change, the more they stay the same.[17] The reason prospects used to pay attention to some of the interruptions from salespeople and marketing teams, was that in a world where there was limited access to information, some of these communications were of value. In other words, by talking about their products or services, salespeople could often provide information of significance to individuals who would be unable to access it easily from elsewhere.

Today, salespeople and marketing teams still need to provide value to prospects, but what has changed is the idea of value itself. Nowadays, if sales or marketing departments only create material that promotes their offering, it is likely to have little worth in a business environment where there are so many similar organizations peddling their wares, and so much information available.

In fact, there are still too many marketers and salespeople trying to use social media platforms purely transactionally, making constant attempts to promote the benefits of their products and services. Using digital channels in the same way as one would have customarily utilized advertising or direct mails will add little value to prospects, and will prove ineffective. Traditionally, media companies would build an audience. Salespeople and marketers would then pay to interrupt that particular group. In the digital environment, however, sales and marketing personnel need to build their own audience. This will not be achieved with the same transactional messaging employed when interrupting people whose attention had been obtained by another organization.

Instead, salespeople and marketing teams need to create value around the products or services that they offer. In essence, what this means is that the communication should have some worth for the prospect, regardless of whether they are in the market to buy at that particular moment. For example, a law firm providing intellectual property services may produce quarterly updated factsheets about how intellectual property law is changing in certain territories around the world, and the implications for businesses. This content could be useful even if an individual had no intention of instructing an intellectual property law firm at that specific time.

If the material is insightful, it allows the intellectual property firm to earn some credibility and trust with potential customers. Moreover, if content regularly produced by the firm is found to be of value, prospects may come to refer to some of it on a regular basis. In this way a couple of things start to happen.

First, this law firm's own view of the market is informing its readers. This being the case, it is extremely likely that when a prospect does come to make a purchase, some of their buying criteria will necessarily match the law firm on which they have been relying for a substantial amount of information. Second, it is unimaginable that an individual, having utilized the content produced by the law firm on a regular basis, would then not consider this firm as one of the possibilities when looking for a supplier. In other words, the regular engagement allows this firm to be in the 'buying set' of the prospects and customers that are consistently using its material.

Creating 'value' around what the company does is important. In other words, the content should relate, in some way, to the products or services the business supplies. The risk, otherwise, is that an organization could engage potential customers and yet never obtain any business.

So, in the example of our intellectual property law firm, the factsheets are informing prospects and customers of the changes occurring in different jurisdictions and the general implications for businesses. While providing value, it pertains to the services the firm offers around registering and protecting patents and trademarks. In the business-to-business world, it is likely that an organization has quite a narrow scope in order for the content it produces to seem relevant to its offering in the mind of the customer.

On the other hand, lifestyle businesses might be able to stretch the range of content they create, and from the customer's viewpoint, still be able to relate it to their offerings. For example, if a leisure company identifies its core deliverable as providing remarkable moments in relation to people's personal lives, it may be able to create content around a wider range of subject areas relevant to individual consumers. This material may still be perceived to be linked to the company's core offering by its clientele.

The other reason a company should be creating 'value' around what it does, is because in the main, it should not give away products or services for which it wishes to charge. Of course, there are exceptions to this rule, but free access to products or services normally devalues them in the mind of the customer and is, therefore, generally not good practice.

So, for example, our intellectual property law firm should not 'give away' free consultancy if ultimately that is a main service for which it wishes to charge. However, packaging up knowledge into factsheets, newsletters or webinars is fine, as this is not directly what the company sells. In a world where information is widely available, providing knowledge enables a business to engage prospects, establish trust and gain credibility. Guarding the expertise a company has is normally futile. Essentially, if an individual does not access the information from one business, they will almost certainly be able to get it from another. Therefore, quite simply, a different organization benefits from the engagement, trust and credibility that sharing knowledge generates.

With the ubiquity of information available today, it is rarely expertise that a knowledge-based business sells. Rather, it is the 'application' of that know-how that people buy. For example, a person could conceivably access enough information to be able to apply to register a trademark. However, knowing the probability of it being accepted, the form in which it should be submitted to make it more likely to go through, the process for appeal should the mark be initially rejected, plus the time this would all take when it is not their core competency, means that for many people, trying to undertake this task themselves would be untenable.

In consequence, our law firm should package its knowledge using mechanisms such as articles, podcasts, videos and webinars etc., which will enable it to attract prospects and build its community. The application of the knowledge, in this case the consultancy itself, should not be given away, as that is one of the main services for which it makes a charge.

By taking this approach, what a company or salesperson is achieving is 'mindshare'. Big brands traditionally paid for mindshare by being 'everywhere' and 'interrupting' us often. Therefore, one could not think of fast food eateries without considering McDonald's, soft drink manufacturers without Coca Cola coming to mind, or instant coffee without Nescafé being one of the labels mentioned. This recognition does not guarantee them any particular individual's business, but it means that they are in the 'buying set' when a purchase is being considered. If every time someone thinks of picking up some fast food McDonald's comes to mind, the likelihood is that McDonald's will 'win' a certain amount of the available business.

Of course, most companies cannot afford to 'pay' for mindshare like some of these big brands, but digital channels allow salespeople and marketing departments to 'earn' mindshare. In other words, by producing content of value and building an audience of prospects, when an individual is ready to buy, the salesperson will be in their buying set. As we have identified, if the prospect is regularly engaged with their content, the salesperson may have very well already influenced the criteria of purchase in their favour. Moreover, in being front of mind, and having built some credibility and trust with the purchaser, the salesperson is more likely to be approached at the 'awareness' and 'interest' stage of the buying journey when they can still add value and influence the buying decision.

As with the example of our intellectual property law firm, ultimately what is achieved in the middle of the funnel is 'mindshare' of the target audience with whom the business wishes to engage. The most precious resource from a sales and marketing perspective today is attention. By attracting prospects into the funnel and retaining them within it, when they are ready to buy, either the individual salesperson or the company will be one of their points of reference. In other words, before a salesperson wins 'share of wallet' they must first obtain 'share of time'.

Whereas salespeople only used to receive a prospect's time as a result of trying to sell to them, today, time is an asset in its own right.

In a world where customers have been empowered, it is those businesses and salespeople that can 'earn' the attention of their market place, even before a purchase is likely to go ahead, that will ultimately succeed. Not only is the salesperson likely to be in the prospect's 'buying set' when they are ready to make a purchase, but through their content, they will have had a chance to educate the customer and build some credibility and trust. This, of course, increases the probability of securing a deal.

Having been able to establish some credibility and trust with a prospect, while being used as an information source, it is more feasible that a salesperson will be invited to enter the purchasing process early enough to really have an impact on the buyer's criteria of purchase. This, together with the benefits that the 'social sharing' of content brings, and the referrals and recommendations that can also transpire, means building an engaged community of prospects and customers is vital in today's digital world.

It is important to distinguish between mindshare that is referred to as 'paid for' and attention that is 'earned'. Quite rightly, someone could point out that by creating content of value an organization is still 'paying' for attention. After all, it costs marketing departments and salespeople time, and therefore money, to produce content that will engage prospects.

The difference, however, is fundamental. Mindshare for which an organization 'pays' is won by interrupting someone else's audience. The cost is a direct one. Traditionally, a business would pay a publisher, or broadcaster, to interrupt the audience that they had built with the content the business had commissioned and created, but the audience wasn't particularly interested in the company paying to interrupt them. Rather, they were engaged with the content produced by the media organization. This meant that an organization had to continually interrupt its target audience in order to be remembered. This could be quite an expensive way of obtaining mindshare.

Of course, there is a cost to marketing departments and individual salespeople creating content. However, the reason that 'earned' mindshare is referred to as such is because prospects engage with the material out of choice. They choose to visit the company's website, access videos on its YouTube channel or read a particular salesperson's blog. If they continue to interact with these platforms over a longer period of time, it is completely their choice and is likely to be due to the fact that they receive real value from the content. This mindshare is being 'earned' as a direct result of creating valuable material. This is in contrast to attention that is 'paid for' when the prospect is interrupted with messages they did not ask for.

The narrowing at the base of the Digital Sales Funnel is where prospects turn into customers. It reflects the fact that, in relative terms, there will be far fewer customers at the bottom of the funnel than there are prospects in the wide middle part.

Of course, once prospects have been turned into customers they then sit outside of the purchase funnel. However, it is strategically important that salespeople, customer service teams or key account managers look after these individuals in order to retain them, obtain repeat business and identify opportunities that may exist for up-selling or cross-selling of products and services. These customers may require different messaging and may receive offers distinct from prospects, but much of the content with which they interacted originally may still be useful and relevant in keeping their attention and maintaining engagement.

Endnotes

1 AIDA: (undated) AIDA marketing, *Wikipedia* [online] https://en.wikipedia. org/wiki/AIDA_%28marketing%29 [accessed 3 February 2016]

   'A – attention (awareness): attract the attention of the customer. I – interest of the customer. D – desire: convince customers that they want and desire the product or service and that it will satisfy their needs. A – action: lead customers towards taking action and/or purchasing.'

2 AIDA concept: (undated) AIDA marketing: *Wikipedia* [online] https:// en.wikipedia.org/wiki/AIDA_%28marketing%29#cite_note-7 [accessed 3 February 2016]

   'The first instance of the AIDA acronym was in an article by C.P. Russell in 1921... C.P. Russell, "How to Write a Sales-Making Letter", Printers' Ink, June 2, 1921.'

3 Elias St. Elmo Lewis: Steve Hall (2013) How inbound marketing aligns with the new purchase loop, *Hubspot.com,* published 8 February [online] http://blog.hubspot.com/blog/tabid/6307/bid/34158/How-Inbound-Marketing-Aligns-With-the-New-Purchase-Loop.aspx [accessed 3 February 2016]

'In 1898, Elias St. Elmo Lewis developed the Purchase Funnel, the now familiar pathway customers travel from consideration to purchase.'

4a William W. Townsend: (undated) Purchase funnel explained, *Everything Explained* [online] http://everything.explained.today/Purchase_funnel/ [accessed 3 February 2016]

'The concept of associating the funnel model with the AIDA concept was first proposed in "Bond Salesmanship" by William W. Townsend in 1924.'

4b Bond Salesmanship: William W. Townsend (1924) *Bond Salesmanship,* H. Holt and Co., New York

5 AIDA acronym: (undated) AIDA marketing, *Wikipedia* [online] https://en.wikipedia.org/wiki/AIDA_%28marketing%29#cite_note-7 [accessed 3 February 2016]

'The first instance of the AIDA acronym was in an article by C.P. Russell in 1921… C.P. Russell, "How to Write a Sales-Making Letter", Printers' Ink, June 2, 1921.'

6 AIDA 1893 concepts: (undated) AIDA marketing – history, *Wikipedia* [online] https://en.wikipedia.org/wiki/AIDA_%28marketing%29#cite_note-7 [accessed 3 February 2016]

'A precursor to Lewis was Joseph Addison Richards (1859–1928), an advertising agent from New York City… In 1893, Richards wrote an advertisement for his business containing virtually all steps from the AIDA model, but without hierarchically ordering the individual elements.'

7 Frank Hutchinson Dukesmith: (undated) AIDA marketing – history, *Wikipedia* [online] https://en.wikipedia.org/wiki/AIDA_%28marketing%29#cite_note-7 [accessed 3 February 2016]

'The first published instance of the general concept, however, was in an article* by Frank Hutchinson Dukesmith (1866–1935) in 1904. Dukesmith's four steps were attention, interest, desire, and conviction…'

*Three natural fields of salesmanship, *Salesmanship* 2(1), January 1904, p. 14

8 Desk phones: Christine Crandell (2014) Why desk phones are never answered, *Forbes /Leadership,* published 4 January [online] http://www.forbes.com/sites/christinecrandell/2014/01/03/why-desk-phones-are-never-answered/#2e3f91837d57 [accessed 3 February 2016]

'In a poll of our clients about how they use their phones, the overwhelming response was "desk phones are for outbound calls only. Cellphones are for inbound calls". This is due to developments such as flexible working and home working.'

9 Phone v Text: Jeffrey Kluger (2012) We never talk any more: the problem with text messaging, *cnn.com,* published 31 August [online] http://edition.cnn.com/2012/08/31/tech/mobile/problem-text-messaging-oms/ [accessed 3 February 2016]

'The telephone call is a dying institution... Americans ages 18–29 send and receive an average of nearly 88 text messages per day, compared to 17 phone calls... even in the 65 and over group, daily texting still edges calling 4.7 to 3.8.'

10 Funnel: David Court, Dave Elzinga, Susan Mulder and Ole Jørgen Vetvik (2009) The consumer decision journey, *McKinsey & Company,* published June [online] http://www.mckinsey.com/insights/marketing_sales/the_consumer_decision_journey [accessed 3 February 2016]

'But today, the funnel concept fails to capture all the touch points and key buying factors resulting from the explosion of product choices and digital channels, coupled with the emergence of an increasingly discerning, well-informed consumer.'

11a Interruptions: Thales S. Teixeira (2014) The rising cost of consumer attention: why you should care, and what you can do about it, working paper, *Harvard Business School,* published 17 January [online] http://www.hbs.edu/faculty/Publication%20Files/14-055_2ef21e7e-7529-4864-b0f0-c64e4169e17f.pdf [accessed 3 February 2016]

'Because consumers control, for the most part, where they allocate attention, marketers should address the first question by understanding what consumers are interested in learning about or experiencing... Otherwise, consumers may disregard the message even before it has a chance of being evaluated.'

11b Interruptions: Andrea Lehr (2016) Consumers weigh in on the efficacy of inbound marketing, *Marketo Blog*, published 6 January, [online] http://blog.marketo.com/2016/01/the-efficacy-of-inbound-marketing.html [accessed 3 February 2016]

'Consumers don't want interruptions, and the ability to block ads has fundamentally changed the consumer/brand relationship. Instead of overly promotional content that has little to no value to them, consumers are looking for brands that offer valuable content – something that ignites a conversation.'

12 Searching online: Kimberlee Morrison (2014) social media has changed how consumers shop online, *Social Times*, published 22 December[online]http://www.adweek.com/socialtimes/social-media-changed-consumers-shop-online-infographic/209738 [accessed 3 February 2016]

'People believe their peers on social media more than ever before. The biggest influencer for holiday shopping was recommendations from friends and family on social media, with 68 per cent of survey participants ranking at the top. Sixty-three per cent were influenced by Amazon reviews, and 24 per cent... by blogger endorsement.'

13 Unsolicited calls: Barbara Giamanco and Kent Gregoire (2012) Tweet me, friend me, make me buy, *Harvard Business Review*, published July–August [online] https://hbr.org/2012/07/tweet-me-friend-me-make-me-buy [accessed 9 October 2015]

'the return on cold calling is dropping with every passing year. Indeed, in a recent survey by InsideView, an online provider of sales-relevant content, more than 90% of C-level executives said they "never" respond to cold calls or e-mail blasts.'

14 Time online: (2015) Time spent online doubles in a decade, *Ofcom*, published 11 May [online] http://media.ofcom.org.uk/news/2015/time-spent-online-doubles-in-a-decade/ [accessed 3 February 2016]

'2014 saw the biggest increase in time spent online in a decade, with internet users spending over three and a half hours longer online each week than they did in 2013 (20 hours and 30 minutes in 2014, compared to 16 hours and 54 minutes in 2013).'

15 Research online: (undated) Kimberlee Morrison (2014) 81% of shoppers conduct online research before buying, *Social Times*, published 28 November [online] http://www.adweek.com/socialtimes/

81-shoppers-conduct-online-research-making-purchase-infographic/208527 [accessed 3 February 2016]

'Eighty-one per cent of shoppers conduct online research before they make a purchase. Sixty per cent begin by using a search engine to find the products they want, and 61 per cent will read product reviews before making any purchase.'

16 Word of Mouth: Brewster Stanislaw (2015) Why social is the new word-of-mouth marketing, and what that means, *MarketingProfs*, published 7 January [online] http://www.marketingprofs.com/opinions/2015/26771/why-social-is-the-new-word-of-mouth-marketing-and-what-that-means [accessed 3 February 2016]

'Word-of-mouth is the oldest, most powerful marketing channel in the history of mankind. It's so old that it was marketing before marketing even existed. We'll always trust the opinions of peers and like-minded individuals over marketing copy geared to make us purchase.'

17 Jean-Baptiste Alphonse Karr: (undated) *Wikipedia* [online] https://en.wikipedia.org/wiki/Jean-Baptiste_Alphonse_Karr [accessed 3 February 2016]

'(24 November 1808 – 29 September 1890) was a French critic, journalist, and novelist. His epigrams are frequently quoted, for example "plus ça change, plus c'est la même chose"... usually translated as "the more things change, the more they stay the same" (Les Guêpes, January 1849).'

Measuring the new Digital Sales Funnel

05

Being able to monitor success is fundamental to any marketing department or sales team. Within the Digital Sales Funnel there are three critical measurements to be considered. They are:

1 How many people are in your funnel?

2 Of the people in your funnel, how many are engaged?

3 How many people are buying?: The return on investment (ROI).

Let's deal with the first. How many people are in your funnel?

The first question to answer is, 'what qualifies as someone being in the funnel?' The response is simple; data capture. Essentially, a salesperson needs to know who individuals are in order to be able to reach out and develop an ongoing engagement with them. For example, if a business has a lot of anonymous visitors to its website, reading its blog or watching its videos, it becomes impossible to proactively attempt to deepen the engagement with any of those people, or track the effectiveness of all the different aspects of the company's sales and marketing activities.

On a website, therefore, an organization should try its best to capture data. Of course, an individual will need to be given a reason in order for them to be prepared to supply their details. Amongst the incentives a company can provide in order to obtain information are offers such as a sign-up for a newsletter or blog, the download of a white paper, entry into a competition or registration for a webinar.

Some sites have content behind a data wall. This works by having a small amount of information that can be accessed freely, allowing a potential user to ascertain the value in the material. There will then be a rich array of further content, for example videos, podcasts, articles, webinars and e-books etc., that cannot be accessed without registering for a type of membership or subscription to the site. This is not necessarily paid – it may very well be free – but it enables the company to capture the details of those using the site.

In all these scenarios there is a simple value exchange taking place. A prospect will have to decide whether the offering from an organization is compelling enough to make them give up some information about themselves. Of course, the more details that are required, the more compelling the offer has to be in the eyes of the customer.

In other words, to provide a name and e-mail address, an individual may need to ensure they will obtain some value from the material. However, if a postal address, company name, job title and phone number are also required, that person is going to expect to receive a lot more value. Moreover, the data exchange has to make sense in the eyes of the customer.

So, in signing people up for a newsletter, asking for a name and e-mail address makes sense. After all, the organization requires these details so as to have somewhere to send the correspondence. However, requesting information such as a postal address, company name, job title and telephone number will most likely seem excessive in the eyes of the person subscribing. Ultimately, none of those details will seem particularly necessary in order to receive the bulletin.

If a business is not obtaining enough sign-ups, despite having a substantial amount of web traffic, then it will have to review whether the value on offer, or calls to action are compelling enough for the data being requested. Of course, the marketing team and salespeople should constantly be testing and measuring the different content they provide to prospects and customers. By continually striving to improve the effectiveness of their output, organizations can get better at obtaining data from web visitors.

As a rule of thumb, and in order to start off some initial engagement, a business does not need to ask for any more details than a name and e-mail address. This is because with an e-mail address, using social CRM software, it is possible to display the social platforms on which an individual has a presence. In this way, a lot more information can be learned about a prospect, without creating a barrier, by asking for it as part of the sign-up process There is more about social CRM in Chapter 9.

Of course, a vast number of visitors to a website will not 'sign up' for whatever value is on offer. Although a business should always be trying to improve its level of sign-ups, salespeople can be proactive in this area. There are a number of companies that provide IP identification software. This enables an organization to identify the individual companies that have visited its website. So, for example, if a company mainly deals with HR managers and HR directors, and a salesperson can see a particular enterprise has visited the company website, then they can deduce that the visitor is very likely to have been the HR manager or director. On that basis, they can make further contact. There is more about IP identification software in Chapter 9.

Although this is a more proactive approach, it still relies on people visiting an organization's website in the first place. Of course, there will be individuals who may have arrived at the website by accident and for whom the offering is not appropriate. However, there will be other visitors who are fact finding and genuinely interested. Just as those signing up for a download, white paper or video etc., show themselves to be engaged with the business and therefore would be counted as a prospect in the funnel, so would these visitors once they have been qualified by a salesperson. In other words, once it is clear that these people are interested, in some way, in the company's offering, they would also be considered a prospect in the sales funnel.

The third type of data that can be captured is from communications that take place on social platforms. Posting valuable content on the appropriate networks will lead to people interacting with you. Whether someone follows you on Twitter, connects on LinkedIn, adds you to a circle on Google+, 'likes' your page on Facebook or chooses to comment on a post, in taking these actions, people reveal themselves to you. With the aid of social CRM and social media monitoring software (which we will cover in Chapter 9) it is possible to make contact and start a dialogue with these individuals.

When reaching out to prospects you must consider the nature of the initial interaction, in order to ensure they are contacted in an appropriate way. So, signing up for a newsletter on a website is a reasonably proactive step for someone to take. If it can be identified that they are regularly engaging with the newsletter, for example by clicking on many of the links contained within it, then inviting them to an appropriate webinar may seem entirely applicable.

Conversely, finding out who an individual is via an IP address means someone chose not to provide details or reveal themselves when visiting the website. Therefore, it may be a case of searching for this individual on a platform such as LinkedIn and attempting to connect. By accepting the invitation, the prospect would provide the salesperson with an opportunity to slowly, and over time, develop a conversation with that individual.

Similarly, 'liking' a page on Facebook is a relatively passive activity. Even commenting on a post could just be because the specific article caught an individual's eye, rather than them being particularly interested in the company's commercial offering. Of course, these activities still present an opportunity to start some engagement and begin to earn mindshare. However, in these scenarios, jumping straight in with an invitation to sign up for a webinar may seem a little overbearing and heavy handed as a first communication. Ultimately, salespeople have always had to exhibit empathy and possess some emotional intelligence in order to be effective. This is as true in the digital environment as it is offline.

Between the data sign-ups obtained from a website, the contacts confirmed via IP addresses and the interactions via social channels, a salesperson or marketing department should be able to assess how many people are in their funnel. However, this figure in itself is meaningless. Too many organizations, and salespeople, collect subscribers, connections and followers without any understanding of how this activity will directly lead to business. Simply amassing Facebook 'likes' or Twitter 'followers' is inconsequential unless these are people and companies with whom genuine business opportunities could exist, and with whom real engagement can be generated. In order for this to happen, salespeople and marketing teams must have a good understanding of the numbers within their target market.

For example, I was once in the office of a business that created software for accountancy practices in the UK. I was explaining the Digital Sales Funnel and the measurements involved. At this juncture the managing director interrupted.

'Well', he said, 'we have 1,000 accountancy firms with a relevant contact in our funnel, isn't that good?'

'I don't know', I replied. At this point the managing director seemed a little frustrated.

'I am not sure you heard me', he responded. 'We have 1,000 accountancy firms with a relevant contact in our funnel, isn't that good?'

'I don't know' I repeated. The managing director was visibly irritated.

'Can I ask you a question?' I requested.

'Yes', said the managing director.

'How many accountancy firms are there in the UK?' I inquired.

'I don't know', replied the managing director, to my absolute amazement.

The point is, that if there are 1,500 accountancy practices in the UK, then having 1,000 with a relevant contact in the funnel is fairly impressive. On the other hand, if there are 10,000 accountancy practices in the UK then it is obviously less notable.

In other words, the number of people in the funnel should not just be an arbitrary figure, simply dependent on getting an ever-increasing amount of sign-ups on a website or connections on social media platforms. Rather, the numbers should be measured against the size of the market.

Let's assume there are in fact approximately 7,000 accountancy firms in the UK.[1] In the case of our software provider, we now have a figure against which we can measure the numbers in our funnel. Having 1,000 relevant firms with a contact in the database represents a little under 15 per cent of the market. Consequently, one of the KPIs of the software company may be to increase that number from 1,000 firms to 2,000 over the course of the following year.

Moreover, as an established business, the software company may be aware that for its product the main protagonists, in the majority of buying journeys, are the senior partner and the practice manager. Therefore, although there are 7,000 firms, there are in fact 14,000 main contacts with whom the software business would wish to engage. These figures will obviously play out differently for every organization or salesperson, but the principle behind this example is true for every business. Whether it is a salesperson working in a particular geographical territory or market sector, or a marketing department responsible for the entire organization's communications, the number of people in the funnel must be measured against the size of the market. In this way, definitive KPIs can be set over a specific timeframe.

Of course, it is important for a company to assess who is in its funnel, for it is quite likely that a business may attract some followers, connections or subscribers who are not part of its defined audience. These individuals, for whatever reason, are still interested in the company or the content it is creating. It is possible that some of these people could end up as clients. Some may become referrers. Their interest may be that they work with a similar group of customers. In essence, it does not matter why they choose to engage. However, a company must constantly assess that the material it is producing is highly targeted for its own market place, and it is not inadvertently missing its own prospects while attracting others.

Of course, when measuring how many people are in the funnel, against the identified market opportunity, those falling outside the target audience cannot be used in the figures. So, in our software provider's situation the 1,000 contacts in its funnel represent senior partners and practice managers of accountancy firms. Any other individuals in the funnel, if not belonging to the target customer group, would be measured separately. Marketing teams and salespeople must be aware of the different followers and subscribers they have within their database.

The more defined the 'who' is, the easier it becomes to create content that, in the main, will appeal to the specific audience with which the company wants to engage. There are always likely to be some other people who choose to interact with the material, for a variety of reasons. However, as long as the content a business is producing is highly relevant and helping to attract the right market, there are no real issues in picking up some other individuals along the way.

For example, if our software provider publishes an article in January, 'Top trends that partners of accountancy firms should be aware of for this year', it might attract some consultants who work with accountants. A couple of lawyers may pick up on the article to see if it has relevance for them. However, it is likely that this content is going to attract more accountants than any other audience, because of the title, the material itself and also on which digital assets it will be placed.

The 'who', however, is even more fundamental to a company's success than simply being able to ascertain the market size. We live in a world today where the USP is fundamentally redundant. The idea behind the USP, or unique selling proposition, was the unique benefit a company could offer that would attract customers.[2]

Today we operate in a market place where, in the main, there is more choice and availability than ever before. Companies are competing globally and speed in itself has now become a competitive advantage. In this environment, it is a tiny amount of businesses that can claim to have a USP.

In services, it is almost impossible to have a USP. In short, there is nothing an organization can propose that cannot be copied. If a competitor deems that they are losing business because of the offering another company provides, they will certainly match the proposition. It may not be delivered as well, but from a communication standpoint, both enterprises will look the same.

Even in products, where it is more conceivable that a USP can be created, it is extremely unlikely. For example, Apple is widely regarded to have reinvented the tablet computer with the launch of the iPad in April 2010.[3] With its touch interface there had never been a tablet computer quite like it before. However, despite its groundbreaking innovation, Apple's first mover advantage was a mere two months, as the Dell Streak was launched in June 2010,[4] closely followed by the Samsung Galaxy Tab in September of the same year.[5]

I am not suggesting that companies should not innovate. Of course, I believe that they should. In fact, in most market sectors, constantly evolving, developing and therefore innovating new products and services is a minimum requirement just to be able to compete with other organizations. However, in today's competitive world, companies do not have the luxury of creating something new, and then capitalizing on it for months or even years before other businesses catch up.

This is not to say that companies cannot differentiate. They absolutely can. However, in today's business environment organizations do not differentiate with USPs, which essentially relate to 'what' they do.

We have already explored, in Chapter 3, the importance of a company having an ethos behind its business. We examined the way in which this purpose will affect 'how' an organization creates its offering. In this way, we saw how Innocent differentiates itself from competitors despite making a product, fruit smoothies, that plenty of other companies supply.

The other key in differentiating a business is to define 'who' the actual customer is, in the most clinical way possible. Again, the 'who' will not necessarily affect 'what' a company offers, but it will change 'how' it is delivered.

We explored in Chapter 2 the way in which the economy is changing. We are now living in an 'experience economy' rather than a product- or service-based one. Experiences are not necessarily informed by 'what' a company does. Rather, an experience is created by 'how' an organization delivers its offering. The 'how' will be greatly influenced by the 'who'. In the digital world these aspects, in many ways, have become more important than the 'what'.

For example, a human resources (HR) consultancy specializes in assisting organizations without a dedicated HR function. It basically provides the same HR advice and assistance as every other HR consultancy. If we assume that the vast majority of practitioners are competent in their role, and taking into consideration that the employment law to which they must adhere is the same for everyone, there will be very little to differentiate between suppliers of the service.

However, this HR firm decided to specialize in only working with manufacturing companies. In so doing, it started to partner with some of the leading manufacturing associations in the UK, contributing content to their websites and blogs and discussing particular issues that were specifically pertinent to this sector.

As the UK is predominantly a service-based economy,[6] there will be HR consultancies that have very little experience of managing some of the challenges related to having a workforce of largely blue collar workers, but our HR consultancy specialized in these issues. It kept abreast of the economic realities of manufacturing, depending on where in the economic cycle the UK was, and ensured it could assist management teams in dealing with some of their commercial realities. The firm attended specific events and ensured all of its content was written in a tone and language that would resonate with its audience.

In short, 'what' the HR consultancy delivers is the same as many other providers. It is advice and practical assistance with regard to recruiting and managing employees, and implementing employment law. However, 'how' they package and deliver the offering has completely changed because of the specific market this firm is addressing. This consultancy is different, and will be much more appealing to the majority of manufacturing companies than most others. It is not differentiating on 'what' it does, but 'who' for and, therefore, consequently, 'how'.

We inhabit a world where marketing teams and salespeople alike need to 'earn mindshare' of their target audience. It is an environment where everyone has a channel, and the best marketers and salespeople a company has are therefore the engaged community that shares, talks and recommends its content as well as its products and services. Consequently, every salesperson and marketing team needs to build a community of engaged prospects and customers around their business.

If a salesperson, or marketing team, only wants to earn the mindshare of senior partners at law firms in London they can be very specific. There will be certain websites and forums they use, events they attend, publications they read and issues with which they are particularly preoccupied at any one time.

If the salesperson then decides they want to engage senior partners at law firms across the UK, it automatically becomes more challenging. There will be a wider number of forums and networks to utilize. There might be local events around the country that play an important part for firms in particular regions. There may be nuances in some of the issues about which they are concerned, as provincial economies may have different challenges.

If the salesperson then decides that, in addition to law firms, senior partners at accountancy practices are also good target prospects, then life becomes even more complicated. There will be many more issues of importance. Even challenges that are the same may be addressed in slightly different terms, using variable language. There will, of course, be many more online networks, forums, groups and events etc., which a salesperson may find it useful to attend. The serendipity that occurs amongst individuals and groups when working in tight markets is continually diluted as the target customer base grows.

Of course, salespeople and companies can attempt to reach any size of target market. However, as the ambition grows so do the resources, time and effort that are required. Therefore, a company, or salesperson, should identify its 'who' as the smallest target market possible, in order to reach its commercial objectives on a sensible market share.

The smaller the target market, the easier it is to get known and obtain mindshare, gain credibility and earn trust. Individuals in particular market sectors and geographical locations are likely to know each other. The conversations and exchange of knowledge and information that take place mean that building a profile is normally simpler the more targeted the niche in which you choose to operate. As the audience widens, more time, effort, money and resources are required. A salesperson or business will obtain more 'bang for their buck', for the time and money invested, the smaller the market place in which they work.

Moreover, the tighter the market, the easier it is to create a 'how' that really resonates with the audience and differentiates the organization. Despite delivering the same HR services as many other consultancies, our HR firm created a 'how' and differentiation by concentrating on working with manufacturing companies. If it were to broaden its offering out to the service sector, it would necessarily have to dilute its 'how', and the differentiation between itself and its competitors would start to erode.

Companies and salespeople are often concerned with specifying their 'who' too definitively. This is because they usually feel it will result in excluding opportunities. In fact, the opposite is true.

Let's say that our HR consultancy did not want to specifically target manufacturing businesses. After all, as the managing director points out, HR law is the same for all companies, and therefore they can work with anyone. The content this firm puts out is now necessarily generic and much blander, as it cannot take a real position in the market if it is attempting to appeal to everyone. Rather than concentrate on attending specific events, networking on particular online forums and working with select industry associations, it now attempts to universally address the whole market. The reality is that, while trying to be 'all things to all people', this HR firm becomes 'nothing to anyone'. It is now the same as every other competitor with no differentiation whatsoever.

The irony is that this HR firm is trying to appeal to everyone in order not to exclude any possible opportunities. However, in reality, it is discriminating 'who' it targets. The fact is the business only has a limited amount of resource, and it cannot reach everyone with whom it can work. Moreover, it cannot work with every company in the country in need of HR advice. It simply isn't big enough, and would be unable to grow quickly enough to meet that demand.

However, instead of discriminating strategically, and in so doing creating differentiation, a compelling 'how', and using its marketing and sales capability to its optimum, it is now selecting prospects randomly. In other words, it is now marketing to everyone and will fail to reach the vast majority of possible customers. This is due to lack of time and resource rather than from any strategic decision. It becomes bland, with no discernible difference from competitors and consequently no alluring 'how'. Moreover, its marketing and sales resources are much less targeted and consequently much more wasteful.

Most organizations struggle to differentiate, deliver a truly compelling offer or create irresistible content that will really engage prospects on their website and social channels. Much of this is because companies refuse to take a position in the market and choose a specific 'who'. They feel they are excluding opportunities when the opposite is true – they become bland and uninteresting like every other competitor.

A good analogy is the news. The news is a commodity. There are a multitude of places from apps to blogs, newspapers, TV and radio etc., where it can be accessed. Imagine a publisher, in the business of news, deciding not to take a position. In order not to alienate readers it decides to literally deliver the facts with no insight, opinion or stance whatsoever. Who would buy those newspapers or magazines? Who would be loyal to those newspapers or magazines?

The point is that most successful newspapers and current affairs magazines do take a position. As a consequence, they provide insights, views and opinions from a particular standpoint. In so doing, they alienate much of the market place, but at the same time they also appeal to a distinct audience. Moreover, even with the most commoditized of products, they differentiate themselves and become interesting. The fact is, in order to become successful no individual, group or company needs to be liked by the majority of people. In fact, they can often be loathed by the masses. It is through a small minority of people loving them, and being loyal to them, that they become successful.

Of course, every company has business targets, which it needs to attain. It should therefore pick the smallest 'who' group possible, while still being able to accomplish its commercial ambitions on a sensible market share.

For example, an IT support business was looking for 'who' to target. There are, of course, many companies that outsource their requirements for the overseeing and maintenance of their IT infrastructure. In theory, therefore, why specialize in any particular field? After all, this IT support business can work with anybody. Of course, this would lead to a lack of differentiation and bland messaging like so many other suppliers in the market. As highlighted, it would also be difficult to 'win' the mindshare of an audience when casting the net so wide.

The first client that the owner of the IT support business happened to win a contract with was a law firm. The legal practice had some specific requirements, and the IT support company made sure it could meet its demands. With a story to tell, it seemed sensible to try to 'win' business with other law firms. As the company grew, it marketed itself as a specialist in working with the legal sector.

A lot of the IT maintenance work was undertaken remotely, via engineers who were spread around the country, covering most regions of England and Wales. Therefore, the IT support company was well positioned to be able to 'win' more business, especially in light of its growing experience in the legal sector.

The one consideration was to ensure the market was big enough to meet its commercial ambitions. Its commercial target was to hit £5 million of revenue with an average contract being worth £25,000. This meant having around 200 contracts.

Therefore, the question asked was, how many law firms were there across England and Wales? If the answer was 1,000, then winning 200 contracts would mean having 20 per cent market share. While possible, it would be a tall order for a relatively small business to achieve that sort of penetration. On the other hand, if there were 100,000 law firms throughout England and Wales, then 200 contracts would represent a mere 0.2 per cent market share. One may have suggested, in this instance, reducing the size of the market. For example, this could be achieved by narrowing the geographical coverage to use marketing and sales resources more efficiently. Over time, of course, the IT support business could widen the regions it covers.

In the event, the IT company ascertained there were a little over 10,000 law firms across England and Wales.[7] In order to meet its targets this meant winning 2 per cent market share, which the owner deemed realistic.

As this IT company grew, and realized its commercial goals, the owner of the business had to make a decision. The company could try to achieve more than 2 per cent market share in order to expand, or alternatively, the business could diversify its offering. At this juncture the owner, whilst still pursuing more business in the legal sector, decided to create a proposition for accountancy practices.

The point is that organizations should always work in the smallest market place they can, while ensuring there is enough opportunity within the market to meet their commercial imperatives.

However, as companies grow, they can diversify as long as it is done in a way that is plausible to the customers they service. Most accountants seemed to accept that a lot of experience within the legal sector made the IT company more than competent in their own area of business. Therefore, the brand extension was credible and consequently commercially feasible.

The other aspect of properly identifying the 'who' is to ensure sales and marketing resources are commensurate with the objectives. I was once with the CEO of a business advisory service for small companies. I asked them if they had defined 'who' their customer was in a definitive way. They confidently told me they gave advice to micro-businesses employing fewer than 10 people. Of course, initially this seems like quite a tight definition. However, there are around 5 million micro businesses in the UK,[8] so I questioned whether the 'who' had been defined well enough. The CEO insisted it had.

I asked another question. I inquired as to the sales and marketing resources the CEO had at their disposal to reach over 5 million potential prospects. They smiled as they acknowledged the ridiculousness of their answer. They told me that Jane works on Tuesdays and Thursdays and her marketing budget, after her salary, was £25,000. There are of course no exact correct ratios, but trying to reach over 5 million people on less than 16 hours a week, and with only £25,000, seemed like an impossible goal.

In fact, many sales and marketing departments are set up to fail, with ambitions that far outreach the resources available for achieving them. In this case, the CEO had two options: increase the sales and marketing capability or narrow the target market. For example, apart from the obvious demarcation by way of geography, companies with one or two employees are quite different from a business with getting on for 10. Therefore, even within this tight market place there was room for further segmentation.

While marketing departments may be making these decisions on a macro scale, salespeople must be doing the same on a team or individual level. With a limited number of hours in the week, salespeople must ensure they are working in tightly defined markets in order to be able to build credibility, earn trust and gain recognition. They should target the smallest market possible, ensuring that while winning a sensible ratio of business, enough opportunity exists, within the area in which they choose to focus, to meet their sales goals.

In a business environment where salespeople have to build an audience, earn mindshare and engage prospects by giving value, the tighter the market place in which they work, the easier this is to achieve and the more differentiated they can become.

When identifying the 'who', all the traditional demographic segmentations should be taken into account. In business-to-business marketing these include geography, market sector, number of employees, turnover, position in the company etc. In business-to-consumer marketing, aspects such as age, gender, marital status, location, income bracket, presence of children etc., should also be taken into consideration.

As well as the traditional segmentations, when examining demographics and choosing the 'who', salespeople and marketing departments should also take into account some other factors. One of these is the prospect's potential to change. Often the biggest barrier to making a sale is not the competition, but rather the 'status quo'. That is, the purchaser ultimately deciding to stay with what they have got and taking no action whatsoever. Purchasers with more potential to change are also more likely to buy.

One aspect of industry, which often exhibits a great potential for change, is sectors that are being disrupted. Therefore, these are frequently good markets to approach. When organizations are unsettled, the 'status quo' is generally not an option. In other words, there can be a recognition that change is inevitable. In this environment, buyers are much more open to using fresh suppliers and embracing new ideas and ways of working.

For example, the launch of Apple's iPad in 2010 completely disrupted the technology sector, with many enterprises having to re-evaluate their plans following the iPad's overwhelming success.[9] Many of these companies were forced to reassess their businesses and change in some way. Continuing on the same path was no longer an option. Therefore, this was potentially a good time to approach the market, depending on the products or services that an organization offered.

Marketing and sales teams should also give psychographics – the characteristics of a person – some attention. These traits such as personality, attitudes, values, interests, lifestyle and behaviours may also inform the 'who'. Sometimes giving psychographics consideration is extremely insightful in choosing 'who' to target and where that audience may be found.

For example, a Cleantech business may be able to identify associations and forums where it is more likely to find prospects whose values align with its own objectives. Of course, this increases the chances of being able to achieve sales down the line.

As marketing teams and salespeople build up their community, social CRM and social media monitoring software can provide an immense amount of understanding as to some of the attitudes, values, interests, lifestyles and behaviours that customers exhibit. This will be explored further in Chapter 9.

Finally, context should also be taken into consideration when identifying the 'who'. That is, what are the circumstances and events taking place that may lead people to look for the type of products or services your company supplies?

Contexts can come in many forms. For example, industry sectors can go through trends where there is a predisposition to look at certain aspects of a business. After the financial crises of 2007–2009, with new regulations being introduced, financial service companies were forced to revisit how they managed their compliance obligations.[10] Therefore, the context of current events provided salespeople and marketing teams with commercial opportunities in this area.

There are contexts that also pertain to individuals. For example, no one wakes up in the morning and decides to look for a new accountant, change their IT supplier or invest in new software on a whim. These purchases always take place within a context. In other words, there will be events or happenings in a business, or in a person's life, that will drive a purchase.

For example, a senior professional may not have ever considered undertaking leadership training or coaching. However, when appointed in their first role as a CEO, and feeling a little overwhelmed, they may decide to see what support is available.

Therefore, a leadership coaching organization may decide its 'who' is not merely CEOs, of which there are many, but rather CEOs in their first year in role. This would inform 'how' they delivered the coaching as well as the content produced. Rather than just create material about how to be a good leader, they may decide to produce literature such as 'how to have an impact in your first 100 days'.

Similarly, people do not generally decide, on impulse, that their senior team requires management training. There are often events taking place in an organization which will lead someone to this conclusion. For example, it could be that there has been increased staff attrition or a particularly high-profile incident that was badly handled. Alternatively, it could be that the business is experiencing high growth, and therefore requires the management team to be able to evolve and step up, as the company develops further. In this context, a management training company may define its 'who' as management teams at high-growth organizations. Again, this would influence 'how' the services are delivered and the type of content that would be created to engage the potential purchasers of the training.

A defined 'who' allows a marketing team or salesperson to use their time and resources in the most effective way possible. Concentrating efforts in a specific market makes it easier to build the mindshare that all marketing departments and salespeople need today in order to be successful. Moreover, having a properly delineated 'who' allows a business to create a compelling 'how'. In so doing a company can truly differentiate itself, creating clear blue water between itself and its competitors.

Understanding how many businesses exist within the defined 'who' is vital, and allows you to measure the first part of the Digital Sales Funnel effectively. First, you can ascertain, from the companies within the funnel, how many are real prospects set against the company's criteria. Second, by understanding the market potential, an organization can set proper KPIs for the first part of the funnel. So, for example, a business might know that within its defined market there are 20,000 companies. If it currently has 5,000 of those in its funnel, then one of the main KPIs that it sets could be to get to 7,500 over the next 12 months.

Once you have defined the answer to how many people are in the funnel, then the second measure becomes appropriate. That is, of the people in the funnel, how many are engaged? Merely collecting prospects into the funnel is, on its own, meaningless. For example, a potential buyer may have visited a website and provided an e-mail address in order to download a report. If, having read the report, there is no more interaction between that person and the organization from which the report came, then there is very little chance of that individual ever becoming a customer.

We live in a world of information overload. This has resulted in it being harder than ever before to obtain the 'attention' of prospects and customers alike. Consequently, from a sales point of view it is more of a challenge to develop a dialogue with prospects, and be able to nurture them through the purchase journey, than in any previous era.

Therefore, what salespeople and marketers need to ensure is that when a potential buyer is ready to make a purchase, their organization ends up in the prospect's buying set. This is achieved through 'mindshare'. Defining 'who' the customer is, in the most targeted way possible, goes some way to assisting in gaining mindshare. This is because it is easier to be known amongst a small group than a huge crowd.

Mindshare can be measured. First, by capturing the data that reveals who has interacted with a business, and second, by surveying the amount of engagement an organization has with these individuals. People will only engage if they are receiving 'value' from the material that a salesperson or marketing department is creating. Regular interaction with this 'value' results in mindshare being obtained and allows credibility and trust to be built. Therefore, this lead nurturing not only ensures a company makes it into its prospect's buying set, but also, having earned some trust and credibility, gives it a good chance of winning the business. Earning mindshare amongst the relevant audience will, over time, deliver quality leads into a business.

Moreover, in a world where everyone has a channel, even those individuals in the funnel who don't buy may turn out to be very good referrers or sharers of content. As the web becomes more social, and searches become increasingly personalized, having the mindshare of a defined audience becomes increasingly important in achieving sales success. The best sales and marketing people a business has today are in the community it builds around its organization.

The first measure we examined is all about data capture and knowing exactly 'who' comes into the funnel. The second measure, therefore, is looking at engagement. In other words, of the prospects in the funnel, how many are engaged?

Why is it that before you get married, traditionally you become engaged? Similarly, if you lock a public toilet in the UK, the outside side of the door often reads 'engaged'. This is because 'engaged' means busy or occupied. Therefore, the question that a salesperson or marketing department must answer is, how many people in the funnel are busy or occupied with me?

Clearly, we would not expect a prospect to be busy with a particular business every day. Therefore, it is up to the marketing team, or salesperson, to decide how often they should 'occupy' their prospect.

Engagement can be measured between any time period: weekly, monthly, bi-monthly, quarterly etc. Ultimately, it depends on the nature of the product or service the business provides, and the value that a salesperson or marketing team is creating beyond their core value proposition.

For example, a supermarket might try to engage a database of prospects every week. This level of engagement might seem unusually high for many businesses, but with the majority of the UK population doing at least one supermarket shop per week, it would not seem unduly onerous for a supermarket to seek this level of engagement.[11]

Meanwhile, a salesperson for a recruitment business might blog once a week, and produce a podcast interviewing an HR expert every other week. With six original pieces of content going out every month, the salesperson may decide to e-mail a newsletter update to prospects twice a month. This is to inform the individuals inside their funnel of the new content that has been produced.

If the content is very insightful, and created for those people who have a major responsibility for recruitment within their organizations, for example HR professionals, then measuring engagement on a monthly basis might be the right frequency. If recruitment is a major part of their job, and a perennial challenge, one would expect this audience to be extremely interested in the material. On the other hand, if the audience consists of small business owners who have many other responsibilities other than recruitment, one might produce appropriate content less frequently and measure engagement every six weeks.

Of course, in order to earn and keep mindshare, it is desirable to engage prospects as often as possible. Short articles, one-minute videos or a few top tips are good ways of delivering great content. This is because it is in small enough nuggets to make it easy for someone to interact with the material, without taking up too much time. It is imperative that a prospect always receives value from the content produced, otherwise they will stop interacting with the material and their attention will be lost.

It really depends on the product or service that a company delivers as to the amount of engagement that can realistically be achieved. There must be a degree of frequency in order to earn and keep mindshare. However, a salesperson or marketing department needs to be careful not to be overzealous with prospects. If people feel they are receiving too much, even if the content is good and valuable, they will feel bombarded and may opt out.

Of course, salespeople and marketing departments have to ensure they are producing enough content to keep people interested. Regularly posting to blogs, putting out tweets, creating videos and contributing to forums etc., are examples of the array of activities required to keep the channels a company or salesperson chooses to use vibrant.

Highlighting new content to prospects via social media messages, or a newsletter, is important. Otherwise, even when people find the material valuable, it is easy for them to forget about it. However, one must be careful with the degree of frequency that direct messages are sent to people in the funnel. There is a balance in ensuring that messages are sent often enough to keep mindshare but not so often that it becomes irritating and overwhelming. There is no prescriptive answer. Much depends on the organization, its offering and the audience with which it is engaged. While many salespeople and marketers will have a natural idea of what frequency feels right, a careful look at the metrics, such as click-through rates and interactions with the material, will provide some evidence on which decisions can be based.

Engagement itself is measured using certain metrics. When sending out a newsletter, all content should be sent as embedded links back to where it is hosted on the website. By doing this it is easy to measure how many people clicked on the links and who they were. Obviously one would consider those individuals that clicked on the links as engaging with the business. This is a more accurate measure than open rates, as many e-mail clients automatically open the next e-mail when the one before it is deleted. In this way, open rates can be misleading. An e-mail that is considered to have been opened, could actually have just been down to a prospect deleting the previous message.

By putting content behind a data wall and having a login to access this material, it is easy to identify returning visitors to the website, and to observe which material they are interacting with. Similarly, cookies will enable an organization to track returning visitors, and therefore in this way be able to determine which prospects in the funnel are engaged.

Social media monitoring software will be able to assist in understanding who may be engaging on social media platforms rather than through any newsletter or on the website directly.

Levels of engagement should be continually measured, so salespeople and marketers can constantly be trying to improve the amount of interaction they have with prospects. So, for example, a salesperson may have 400 prospects in their funnel. Measuring engagement on a monthly basis they may observe that between their blog, social media channels and the website, they have 200 prospects regularly engaged. Therefore, by looking at the content that is most utilized and shared, the timing of when it is posted and the context around which that content is created, salespeople should be assessing how they can improve their levels of engagement.

We inhabit a world where customers have been empowered, and cold calling is becoming less and less effective. Therefore, producing content aimed at defined audiences, on the platforms they use, is a powerful way of winning attention and starting a dialogue with possible buyers. If value is created for prospects they will choose to interact with a particular organization or salesperson. Keeping the prospect engaged allows a salesperson to earn mindshare and thus makes it likely that when an individual is ready to buy, the salesperson or organization will be in their buying set. Moreover, in a world where everyone has a channel and information is increasingly disseminated via social sharing, achieving mindshare of prospects is likely to lead to other referrals and recommendations. These may come directly, or as a result of content being shared.

In the past, selling was undertaken in a very transactional way. Prospects would be interrupted in an attempt to win their attention, and the few who expressed an interest would then be followed up. Salespeople would constantly screen individuals throughout the process until a few became customers.

Interrupting people for attention is less viable than it has ever been. However, winning attention and keeping it, by providing value, is an effective way of prospecting today. In the past, salespeople would only be able to manage a few prospects at any one time. As each one required individual phone calls, meetings and correspondence etc., there would only be a certain volume in the pipeline with which a salesperson could cope.

We have already indicated the importance of salespeople working in tight markets and really defining 'who' they wish to target. However, producing content allows a salesperson to earn the mindshare of many more prospects than they would have been able to in a previous era.

It doesn't make any difference to a salesperson's time whether 150 people or 200 people read their blog. Ultimately, within the salesperson's target market, the more the better.

Of course, among the prospects with whom attention is won, there will be those who, having accessed some content, express a further interest in a company's products or services. At this juncture, a salesperson will look to move the prospect towards a purchase through e-mails, phone calls, meetings etc. Therefore, while a majority of people in the middle of the funnel may have simply indicated an interest in an organization's expertise, there will be prospects who are ready to go further down the buying journey.

By earning the mindshare of potential buyers, salespeople will receive many of these enquiries automatically. However, in constantly looking through the analytics and customer records, salespeople will be able to identify when prospects are interacting more with the website, accessing an increasing amount of information or delving into more granular details such as pricing. When a salesperson notices these behaviours, they can of course reach out to the prospect to see if they can be of more assistance.

Moreover, as in the traditional model of selling, salespeople will be able to keep statistics which, over time, will become incredibly reliable. For example, a salesperson may know that 5 per cent of their engaged funnel will buy in any 12-month period. Therefore, as the middle of the funnel builds they may be able to improve sales figures year on year.

They may also be able to identify those individuals who are good referrers or share content regularly. In this way, it may be possible to engage people on platforms and in networks where more of these types of individuals may be present. For example, a salesperson working for a compliance business, specifically within the financial services sector, may notice that their best referrers and content distributors are accountants. In this scenario the salesperson may deliberately aim some of their material at accountants, and endeavour to get this placed on relevant forums and websites that accountants use.

It might also be possible to measure the relationship between content produced, and the number of prospects being attracted into the funnel. In other words, to what extent does a salesperson notice a correlation between the number of times they post content and how this directly leads to increased interaction on the company's website or social channels? Of course, this will vary amongst target audiences and market sectors. As in all sales, continued measurement of all the metrics will provide a greater understanding of the actions that lead to success. This will enable salespeople to take more control of the sales process as time goes on.

This brings us to the last measure, which is obviously the return on investment or ROI. The question to be asked is, of the people in the middle of the Digital Sales Funnel, how many are buying? The narrow base of the funnel represents the fact that it will be a relatively small percentage of individuals who buy, compared with those engaging in the middle of the funnel. Of course, this is a figure that can constantly be measured, and that all salespeople and marketing teams will strive to improve. For those individuals handling customers post sale, another key question will be, 'Can I get these individuals to buy more, and with greater frequency?'

Understanding metrics such as the average time between when someone enters the Digital Sales Funnel and when they convert, will provide a greater grasp of the purchase journey. Analysing the content with which they engage, the challenges they had and the context in which these occurred is all helpful in gaining a better insight into customer behaviour. It is this awareness and knowledge that enables improvements to be made. The digital environment allows for a lot of data to be collected from which intelligence can be gleaned. Individuals should be constantly reviewing their numbers and looking to improve different aspects of their sales activity in order to be able to continually deliver better results.

Endnotes

1 Accountancy firms: (2015) Key facts and trends in the accountancy profession, *FRC.org*, published June [online] https://www.frc.org.uk/Our-Work/Publications/Professional-Oversight/Key-Facts-and-Trends-in-the-Accountancy-Profes-%281%29.pdf [accessed 4 February 2016]

   'The overall number of registered audit firms was 6,622 as at the 31 December 2014.'

2 USP: Unique selling proposition (undated) *Wikipedia* [online] http://en. wikipedia.org/wiki/Unique_selling_proposition [accessed 4 February 2016]

'*The Unique Selling Proposition... is a marketing concept that was first proposed as a theory to explain a pattern among successful advertising campaigns of the early 1940s. It states that such campaigns made unique propositions to the customer... The term was invented by Rosser Reeves of Ted Bates & Company.*'

3 iPad launch: Apple launches iPad: *apple.com* [online] http://www.apple. com/pr/library/2010/01/27Apple-Launches-iPad.html [accessed 4 February 2016]

'*SAN FRANCISCO – January 27, 2010 – Apple® today introduced iPad, a revolutionary device for browsing the web, reading and sending email, enjoying photos, watching videos, listening to music, playing games, reading e-books and much more.*'

4 Dell Streak: (2010) Press releases: *Dell.com*, published 25 May [online] http://www.dell.com/learn/us/en/uscorp1/press-releases/2010-05-25-dell-streak [accessed 4 February 2016]

'*Date: 5/25/2010 – Bracknell, United Kingdom – Streak to launch early June in the UK exclusively on O2.*'

5 Samsung Galaxy Tab: Paul Miller (2010) Samsung Galaxy Tab preview, *Engadget*, published 2 September [online] http://www.engadget. com/2010/09/02/samsung-galaxy-tab-preview/ [accessed 4 February 2016]

'*Full PR text: London, UK, September 2, 2010 – Samsung Electronics Co., Ltd, a global leader in mobile technology, today announced the launch of the Samsung GALAXY Tab (GT-P1000)... the GALAXY Tab is the first of the company's tablet devices, representing a new category of mobile products for Samsung.*'

6 Service economy: Andrew Sentance (2013) UK economy: it's rebalancing – but not as we know it, *Telegraph*, published 2 November [online] http://www.telegraph.co.uk/finance/comment/10422712/ UK-economy-its-rebalancing-but-not-as-we-know-it.html [accessed 4 February 2016]

'*Services make up about 80pc of output and employment in the UK, spanning a very diverse range of activities – including financial and business services, transport and communications, health, education, social care, retail, hotels and catering.*'

7 Law firms: Author (2013) Number of law firms dips to new low, *Law Society Gazette,* published 31 October [online] http://www.lawgazette.co.uk/practice/number-of-law-firms-dips-to-new-low/5038472.fullarticle [accessed 4 February 2016]

'*According to figures from the Solicitors Regulation Authority, there were 10,726 practising firms in England and Wales.*'

8 Micro businesses: (undated) Business Population Estimates for the UK and Regions in 2015, *National Federation of Self Employed & Small Businesses Limited* [online] http://www.fsb.org.uk/media-centre/small-business-statistics [accessed 4 February 2016]

'*There were a record 5.4 million private sector businesses at the start of 2015.*'

9 iPad re-evaluation: Rene Ritchie (2014) History of iPad (original) Apple makes the tablet magical and revolutionary, *iMore.com*, published 6 October [online] http://www.imore.com/history-ipad-2010 [accessed 4 February 2016]

'*Galaxy Tab running stretched out smartphone software.*'

10 Financial Crisis: (undated) Financial crisis of 2007–08, *Wikipedia* [online] https://en.wikipedia.org/wiki/Financial_crisis_of_2007%E2%80%9308 [accessed 4 February 2016]

'*In the immediate aftermath of the financial crisis palliative monetary and fiscal policies were adopted to lessen the shock to the economy.*'

11 Supermarket shop: (2014) SMG UK, Mumsnet survey: Supermarket shopping habits reveal erosion of loyalty, *SMG Source*, published 23 October [online] http://blog.smvgroup.com/smg-uk-mumsnet-survey-supermarket-shopping-habits-reveal-erosion-of-loyalty/ [accessed 4 February 2016]

'*Mums now shop at an average of three supermarkets a week for their main shop.*'

Creating value – the how and why of content

06

Creating value means that the content that is produced has to be interesting to potential buyers, whether or not they are currently in the market to make a purchase. For example, my website stickymarketing.com contains a rich array of videos and articles. You do not have to be looking to use the services of a sales and marketing speaker, or consultant, to obtain value from the site. However, if an individual found the materials on the website useful, and consequently engaged with the content regularly, then it is very likely that if they ever did require a speaker or consultant in the area of sales and marketing, then I would be in their buying set.

Similarly, there is a real estate agency I know of that works with the more affluent homeowners in its area. This agency produces a quarterly report on what is happening within the local housing market, how prices have fluctuated and the current value of different homes, taking into consideration prevailing sales. This report is extremely targeted, created solely for the higher-net-worth individuals this agency serves. By using examples of certain houses, in particular streets, the bulletin gives people a really good sense of present market conditions. It makes it easy to extrapolate a rough idea of what any house, at the upper end of the market, is currently worth.

You do not need to be attempting to buy or sell a house to find this information captivating. With so much of their net worth tied up in their homes, most people are interested in keeping a reckoning of the current price of their property. Knowing present market conditions is useful and means that, when people are thinking about the possibility of moving, they can make a more informed decision in terms of timing. Therefore, for the many subscribers to this report, it provides tremendous value with no requirement for any transaction to occur. Of course, it is very likely that when someone is ready to buy or sell, having read the report regularly, that this real estate agency will be in the prospect's buying set.

In order to attract potential buyers into the top of the funnel, and to keep them engaged in the middle, salespeople and companies alike have to provide them with value. Prospecting in traditional sales and marketing was transactional. Companies paid to interrupt individuals with their marketing messages that were designed to entice people into considering a purchase. Similarly, salespeople would knock on doors and bash away at the phones looking for those parties that were interested in their products and services. In other words, the interruptions that prospects endured were only of value if they were interested in the offer being promoted at that moment. If they were not, these interruptions were a waste of their time.

Being so direct, the transactional approach to sales and marketing, although increasingly ineffective, seems purposeful. On the other hand, producing content to attract prospects into the funnel can feel insufficient. This is because it is a less straightforward route into a potential buyer's consciousness. Simply creating value, though, is not enough. Salespeople cannot afford to constantly be providing potential prospects with content without knowing how it is going to lead to sales down the line. After all, this book is called Digital Selling and not Digital Publishing, and for this there is a reason.

In terms of measuring the effectiveness of content, we must think back to the previous chapter. It is vital that all material is tested and measured. In a digital environment, we can ascertain how often a piece of content was clicked on and how many times it is shared. It is also possible to analyse the information that buyers engaged with on their journey to making a purchase. In this way, salespeople and marketing departments can obtain a really good understanding of the material that is effective and the content that is perhaps less useful. However, with all the testing and measuring in place, salespeople then need to understand the different types of content that are more likely to attract prospects into their funnel and engage them over a period of time.

The first area of content creation to be aware of is the importance of visuals. In a world where we are bombarded with information, and where attention is scarce, perhaps the most significant aspect of visuals is their immediacy. The brain processes images much faster than text, and consequently, they have a direct impact, quicker than the written word ever could.[1]

Therefore, in a world where political views are governed by sound-bites, communications are often limited to short text messages and no one ever seems to have enough hours in the day, visual communications provide a way of cutting through the noise and conveying a lot of information quickly. Basically, it is the fastest way to draw people in and deliver a message.

As a result, even non-visual communications such as an article, blog or white paper should be accompanied by some imagery. Articles with images receive 94 per cent more views than those without.[2] Moreover, visual content is 40 times more likely to be shared on social networks.[3]

With the ubiquity of smartphones today, an increasing number of people are now constantly walking around in possession of extremely powerful cameras and video recorders.[4] These are able to capture and share images and moments in an instant. The emergence and growth of social platforms such as Pinterest, Instagram and Snapchat, shows the power and popularity of sharing visuals.[5]

We have been witness to Facebook becoming increasingly visual over the years. In fact, Facebook is now one of the largest photo-sharing sites on the web.[6] Twitter has also evolved into a very visual platform. For example, in 2012 it bought Vine, even before it was launched, in order to encourage the sharing of short video clips on its site.[7] Meanwhile, 2015 also saw the introduction of both Meerkat[8] and Periscope,[9] apps that enable users to broadcast live video streams from their mobile device.

The fact that the web has become an increasingly visual medium is supported by the simple biological facts:

- 90 per cent of information transmitted to the brain is visual;[10]

- 70 per cent of sensory receptors are in your eyes;[11]

- 50 per cent of the brain is active in visual processing.[12]

This means that salespeople and marketing departments should be aware of the array of visual content options available to them. The most important of these is video.

Fifty per cent of all online mobile traffic is now video.[13] In many ways this makes perfect sense; it is often easier to watch something on a smartphone than to scroll down in order to read a particular item. More generally, 78 per cent of people already watch videos online every week,[14] and many experts expect video to represent 79 per cent of all consumer internet traffic by 2018.[15] Of course, these trends will affect those in the business-to-business arena as well. Already 75 per cent of business executives claim to watch work-related videos every week and this is only likely to increase over time.[16] Moreover, 54 per cent of senior executives share work-related videos on a weekly basis.[17] In essence, video should be a vital part of any content strategy.

Of course, video is not the only visual content that people are able to create. Other useful options include:

- **Photos/pictures/images.** As the web increasingly becomes a visual medium, the importance of photos, pictures and images cannot be underestimated. These should be added to written pieces in order to increase the views and shares they receive. Of course, these images and photos themselves can convey a message. As the character Bazarov stated in Ivan Turgenev's 1862 book *Fathers and Sons*, 'The drawing shows me at one glance what might be spread over ten pages in a book'.[18] In an age of attention deficit, this provides a compelling reason for using images.

- **Infographics.** Of course, these are not new. In fact, cave paintings from over 30,000 years ago could easily be considered the first ever infographics.[19] However, they are a great way of communicating complex ideas and information, often making facts quick and easy to understand. The ubiquity of available online tools enabling individuals to easily develop their own infographics has now made creating them an endeavour in which most people can participate.

- **Presentations.** Creating powerful slide presentations is a very useful way of telling a story and being able to communicate quite complex ideas in an easily digestible format.

- **Memes.** A meme is an image, video or text that is copied, but changed slightly in order to convey an idea. For example, well-known clips from films will often be used. By adding your own captions, the pictures and scenes can take on a whole new meaning. It is their ability to move people emotionally, normally via humour but sometimes by being shocking or insightful, that means they are often widely shared and quickly spread.

- **Screenshots.** These provide a way of communicating complex ideas, and of course can enable someone to demonstrate what something looks like without the requirement of any written description.

- **Image quote cards.** Great quotes are a useful means for conveying an idea. They are often an effective way of communicating a complex message in a simple manner. Quote cards simply take a quote and make it part of a visual, almost like a picture postcard.

- **Cartoons.** The modern use of the term cartoon, normally referring to a humorous illustration, was coined by the British magazine *Punch* in 1843.[20] They are an excellent way of conveying an idea or insight.

- **GIF.** The Graphics Interchange Format is a graphic image on a web page. It is normally used as an endlessly looping few seconds of animation. It is a great way of communicating a message and is a good means for placing content in social networks.

- **Cinemagraph.** This is a GIF where an image is static and just one part has motion. For example, a frame of people on a beach on a windy day may be a still image apart from a flag moving in the wind. It looks like a photograph, with one small part moving, and can be an extremely captivating visual.

While keeping in mind just how important visuals are, it is useful to have some framework for creating compelling content. It can be handy to think of the material in terms of the five Fs: facts, freedom, fortune, fun and fame. Although this is not an exhaustive list, it can provide a good foundation for enabling ideas to come to the fore.

Facts – means delivering really insightful and interesting information. Simply relaying material that is repeated incessantly elsewhere is not valuable. Sometimes it is not merely the knowledge itself that is beneficial, it is the application of it to a particular audience or market place that gives it a fresh pertinence. Examples of types of factual content include:

- Guides – these are normally detailed and lengthy pieces of content.
- E-books/audio books – allow topics to be covered in more depth.
- Case studies – can be in short or long form but are designed to provide insight into the possibilities available to customers.
- Podcasts – an audio file that can be accessed on the move, for example when driving.
- Interviews – often a great way of communicating insights.
- White papers – these are normally technical and detailed pieces of information.
- Webinars – should be kept short. They are a great way of creating an online event people can sign up to. However, they can then be accessed after the recording to provide lasting value.
- E-learning modules – normally interactive, these are an excellent way of communicating ideas and knowledge.
- Newsletters – a useful mechanism for communicating with prospects and existing customers on a frequent basis. This is as long as they provide good value for the recipient.
- Polls and surveys – these can be beneficial in creating new research and insights, and developing a fresh story or angle with which to go to market.
- Reports – an insight-led, longer form of content.
- Blogs and articles – should be kept short. They should make people think and deliver readers a greater understanding on a particular topic.

Freedom – is about convenience. That is, delivering any content that can make people's lives quicker and easier. For example:

– Reviews – allow people to access the knowledge of others to enable them to make decisions, without perhaps having to undertake all the research and forms of inquiry themselves.

– How to's – are a very popular content format. They provide a step-by-step guide to achieving a particular task or outcome, allowing an individual to shortcut some of the learning themselves.

– Lists – 'top five' and 'top 10' checklists enable people to take shortcuts and distil down the multitude of choice, in any field, to a reliable and manageable group.

– Frequently asked questions (FAQs) – provides important information, in an easy-to-digest questions and answers setup.

– Templates – a pre-formatted document that allows an individual to undertake a task in a quicker manner than would have otherwise been possible.

– Resources/tools – providing tools that enable individuals to engage in particular tasks, or shortcuts to the relevant available resources, can save people time and research.

Fortune – the chance to win money or a prize can often be a very effective way of attracting an audience. Although people often associate these techniques with business-to-consumer marketing, companies will enter competitions in order to win accolades. For example, the many business awards that exist often attract organizations that not only benefit from any monetary reward, but can also find the positive publicity they receive invaluable. This content category normally takes the form of quizzes, contests, competitions and awards.

Fun – making communications fun can often be a very effective way of communicating a message that, in another context, would be ignored. For example, 'Dumb Ways to Die' was a public safety video created to promote rail safety for Metro Trains in Melbourne, Australia. It has now been viewed more than 120 million times.[21] The 'Dollar Shave Club' video is an outright sales pitch, but by being delivered in such an entertaining way, not only was it tolerated, but it has received over 21 million views on YouTube.[22] Although it is unequivocally a sales video, it is so entertaining it provides value even for those who have no intention of joining the club.

Another way of making content fun, or certainly compelling, is through gamification. This is basically the idea of using game mechanics and design techniques in non-gaming contexts. By using features such as point scoring and competition with others, people can be encouraged to engage with particular material. For example, the Nike+ Running App[23] encourages individuals to see how their performance stacks up against friends in terms of distance, pace and time etc. Of course, this is a great way for Nike to earn mindshare and stay engaged with its audience.

Fame – we inhabit a world where everyone has the opportunity to own their own media channels, and can contribute opinions and comments that can resonate far beyond a few friends and family. This, coupled with a general fascination with celebrity culture, means that many people aspire to have their moment in the spotlight. For individuals, winning a contest or being recognized for a particular talent can be gratifying in itself. In business, receiving an award or recognition of an achievement can also bring with it commercial advantages.

When referring to the development and distribution of all the different types of material just mentioned, the phrase 'content marketing' is in common use. While it is evident that both salespeople and marketing departments need to be producing content, the terminology is, in itself, unhelpful. The expression 'content marketing' makes it sound like content, in and of itself, is a virtue and that somehow, producing compelling material is, in itself, a meritorious activity. Of course, this is not the case.

'Content marketing' is an outcome of the fact that today both companies and salespeople possess their own channels. Whether it is a website, blog, YouTube channel, Facebook page, LinkedIn profile or Twitter account, both individuals and organizations alike control media channels. However, a channel is only as good as the content it purveys. The BBC is simply a set of cables with a licence to broadcast. What makes it special, or not, is the content it places onto the channels it owns. This is exactly the same for every business and salesperson.

Therefore, if someone decided to opt out and not participate in the digital space at all, they would not require content, because they would not own any channels. Of course, as we have experienced in previous chapters, with an increasing amount of research, recommendations and decision making going online, companies today have to ensure they have a strong web presence in order to be able to compete and succeed.

Inadvertently, this means that every organization has become a media business. As well as supplying whatever the company offers, it now owns media channels that need to be used effectively and require proper management. This is often where marketing and sales begin to go wrong. Generally, salespeople and marketers don't think of the communications they are undertaking as managing a media business, which, in fact, is exactly what it is.

Every salesperson, from a prospecting viewpoint, and every marketer, from a communications angle, should ensure that they are prepared to manage the media side of their activities. First of all, this means being organized.

Each salesperson and marketing team should create for themselves a yearly media calendar. All relevant events, for the geographical locations in which the salesperson or marketing team are operating, should be written onto the calendar. This includes happenings such as public holidays, school vacations, sporting occasions (for example the football World Cup, Super Bowl or the Olympic games), political matters such as elections, and any nationally big TV shows etc. Of course, relevant industry affairs such as key exhibitions and conferences should also be captured.

In this way, marketers and salespeople can start to plan the year and create content that is likely to resonate with their audience. While some of the material that is utilized will be spontaneous, reacting to particular stories, experiences and news, a lot of content can be planned well in advance. Having a content calendar allows individuals to take greater control over their content strategy. Everyone has moments when they are less busy than at other periods. This time can be used to create a certain amount of material, which can then be used at a later date.

If you pick up the latest issue of a magazine, it will always seem current. This is because it is likely to be covering stories that touch on recent events and happenings in whatever industry or subject the magazine is about. However, much of the material will be planned. Interviews with key personnel, competitions, quizzes, spotlights on particular people or topics etc., can all be prepared way in advance and interspersed with up-to-date stories.

The biggest offence in sales and marketing today is to be irrelevant. We live in a world where everyone is constantly bombarded with information and messages. Consequently, in order to be able to cope we are personalizing our communications as much as possible. For example, people assign specific ring tones to certain individuals and use phone number recognition in order to decide whether they should answer the telephone or not. Albums are edited so individuals only have to download and stream songs that they enjoy. Spam filters and prioritized feeds are utilized in order to ensure people only see the messages that are necessary in their e-mail clients or on social media platforms.

The more information we are exposed to, the more vital it becomes to personalize the media with which we interact. Consequently, in this environment, we are becoming less tolerant of irrelevant messaging. Having a calendar of significant events allows salespeople and marketers to utilize those occurrences that are likely to capture the imagination of their prospects and customers.

For example, several years ago I was asked to write an article for an accountancy magazine about marketing. At the time, the UK was hooked on *The X Factor* with the final attracting close to 20 million viewers.[24] If close to 20 million people were watching *The X Factor*, then, by definition, accountants were watching the show. The article I wrote was entitled 'What *The X Factor* can teach accountants about marketing'. At the time, it was the most read article on this particular magazine's online portal.

I would suggest that a large number of accountants are not necessarily interested in marketing. Moreover, there is no reason why an article on marketing should be more interesting than the many other subjects covered on the portal at the time. However, if you were an accountant who watched *The X Factor*, then this article had an immediate relevance and resonance. If the themes of *The X Factor*, marketing and accountancy were weaved together well, then there was a good chance that accountants would share the piece with other colleagues who also liked the show.

Dan Zarella called this technique 'combined relevance'.[25] That is, taking an issue or subject matter you want to inform your audience about and combining it with something your market place is most likely to have an interest in. In this way, the material is immediately relevant and appealing.

Using a calendar enables marketers and salespeople to observe the events that are taking place in any given year. They can then decide if there are some that would resonate with their audience and that they can leverage to pique their interest.

A similar technique, although one which cannot be planned for in the same way, is called 'newsjacking'. Essentially, this means piggy backing off a current news story that is capturing people's imagination, and so is most likely resonating with the audience you want to attract.

For example, during the 2013 Super Bowl between the San Francisco 49ers and the Baltimore Ravens there was a power outage in some parts of the Superdome.[26] It stopped the game for over 30 minutes. Obviously, if a lack of power interrupts one of the biggest sporting events in the world, it is a big story. During that time, Oreo posted an image of a cookie on Twitter with the tagline 'you can still dunk in the dark'.[27] The post was retweeted thousands of times and became a story in itself. This is a classic example of 'newsjacking'. That is, taking a current event or story and leveraging it in some humorous or insightful way.

With a calendar of events in place, salespeople and marketers should then break down activities into daily, weekly, monthly and quarterly tasks. For example:

- Daily – respond to messages and post on Twitter, Facebook or LinkedIn.
- Mondays and Thursdays – publish a new blog.
- Weekly – participate in at least one relevant forum.
- Twice a month (every other week) – post a new video.
- Monthly – release a customer case study.
- Quarterly – run a webinar.

Of course, this example is not meant to be prescriptive. The number of posts, articles, blogs and videos etc., that need to be produced will vary widely depending on the organization, the market and the audience.

The point is, the output needs to be planned in the same way as a media organization would organize and prepare material. This is necessarily undertaken in advance, with the company knowing when certain material will be published or broadcast. Everything can then be tested and measured. What content do people respond to and which has less resonance? Are there better times of the day and days of the week to post certain content formats? What content is the most engaging? What pieces get shared more widely? Looking back, what was the content actual buyers engaged with? In this way, the effectiveness of the materials can constantly be tested, measured and improved.

One of the big challenges that all salespeople and marketers have is time. How is it possible to create the amount of material that is necessary when there are so many other tasks to be undertaken? Of course, marketers would previously put a lot of effort into project managing marketing campaigns, some of which should now be replaced by managing the company media channels. Moreover, salespeople would spend an inordinate amount of their working life cold calling and searching for leads. Again, a lot of this time can be given over to online activities.

Nevertheless, there is no doubt that marketers and salespeople have to work smart in order to manage the stream of content required to be effective on digital channels. Utilization of time and effort is important.

First, it is essential to ensure that there are continually new content ideas. Salespeople and marketers should make it their job to always be switched on to suggestions that may come their way in any given day. This being the case, it is important that they have a system to capture them. Whether this is to use voice recording on their phone, make a note on a phone or tablet, or even in an old-fashioned notebook, it is imperative that these ideas are not lost.

Ideas can come from anywhere. Online, one can read the conversations taking place in forums. People can look at a variety of relevant posts and observe the comments and discourse that these provoke. Following topics on appropriate social platforms can also be insightful and present different thoughts that might be useful, as can reading associated articles and blog posts.

Listing the various challenges different types of customers experience, and listening in meetings to the variety of situations confronting prospects and customers, can provide rich sources of content. The questions prospects and customers ask can also provide a fertile source of ideas. If a prospect asks a thought-provoking question, there is a good chance others are asking it as well. Creating an article, podcast or video around the issue can be a very effective way of producing material that has a real value to both prospects and customers alike.

Thinking about the contexts in which these challenges occur can also provide ideas. Most considered purchases are triggered by an event. For example, the purchase of a new fridge can be because the old one broke, a new kitchen is being installed, people are moving house, or a growing family requires more space. All these different contexts can afford opportunities to create relevant and insightful content for each particular circumstance.

The challenge is blocking off a Monday morning to produce a blog, and then not knowing what to write. By constantly capturing ideas, there will always be a concept available during the times that are designated for content creation.

In the main, it is more efficient to create a lot of content in one go and then drip-feed it out over a few weeks. While times do change, and you would be unable to create content years in advance, most content could be created weeks or sometimes even a few months before it necessarily sees the light of day.

For example, if you commit to posting a blog twice a week, trying to find the time to write these articles on a weekly basis becomes enormously challenging. On the other hand, you may be able to block out a half day in the diary, and write four short pieces in one go. This is normally a more manageable, efficient and reliable way of creating content. Perhaps the most extreme example of this is with video.

As video becomes increasingly important, individuals and organizations need to identify ways of producing a number of videos in the most cost-effective and time-efficient way. I often recommend to clients that they assign one day in the diary, hire a studio or quiet hotel conference room and book a video production company. For the right businesses, interviews are a fantastic mechanism for conveying insightful information in an interesting way. Also, while many people struggle speaking straight to camera, most can come across well when they are being interviewed on a subject about which they possess considerable expertise.

A number of people can be invited to come to the video shoot and should be scheduled for different times of the day. These might include members of staff, customers, suppliers, industry experts or independent consultants – in fact any non-competing businesses or individuals that would be credible, and have a relevant view and interesting angle in relation to the company offering. Of course, the videos have to cover subjects that would be of interest to prospects and customers, but this can be planned in advance.

Each video should only be a few minutes long. It is perfectly possible to create a vast amount of videos in one sitting. Using this technique, I have often finished the day with between 30 and 50 videos, which can then be posted over a six-month period. In this way, for only two days a year, virtually all the video material that is required can be realized. Of course, more creative video pieces such as animations, 'how to' films and others are useful, and I would advocate having a mix of different content if possible.

However, this technique demonstrates how a volume of content can be created efficiently and in a way that is manageable. Content creation is a way of thinking, and once in this mindset it is not nearly as daunting as it first appears.

To further prove this ethos, these videos can then be given to a copy-writer who can use the nuggets of information to create a number of articles and blogs. These articles could then be given to an actor or actress to record, and they can then be utilized as podcasts. In other words, in return for some careful planning and two days during the year undertaking a video shoot, it is perfectly possible for an individual or business to come out with 100 or more pieces of content.

As well as creating their own content, salespeople and marketing departments should also be commissioning material. That is, asking industry experts, recognized leaders, outside consultants and other suppliers to provide articles, podcasts, white papers and videos etc.

As the engaged audience of a salesperson or business grows, people are often very willing to take advantage of the exposure they will receive by producing some material for a website, blog or social media platform. Not only is this a way of obtaining more content, but it usually makes the channel more interesting and credible by containing opinions and views from other experts.

Curation is also a useful way of delivering more content to your own audience of prospects and customers. The term comes from museum curators who, because of their expertise, have the ability to arrange artefacts in an interesting way that often tells a story and provides the visitor with insight. Content curation should happen in exactly the same way.

With both expertise in the subject area and an understanding of their audience, salespeople and marketers should be able to curate content that provides insight, knowledge, and gives value. Introducing the content by way of an opening paragraph, picking out particularly salient points or aspects of the material, or providing a different angle to the story, are all ways that as a content curator, a salesperson or marketing department can provide real benefit. And without having to develop the content in the first place, curation can be a quick and effective way of bulking up a content offering and ensuring some fresh material is posted without always having to be involved in its creation.

Endnotes

1 Images faster than text: Anne Trafton (2014) In the blink of an eye, *MIT News*, published 16 January [online] http://news.mit.edu/2014/ in-the-blink-of-an-eye-0116 [accessed 24 February 2016]

'a team of neuroscientists from MIT has found that the human brain can process entire images that the eye sees for as little as 13 milliseconds – the first evidence of such rapid processing speed.'

2 Articles with images: Jeff Bullas (2012) 6 powerful reasons why you should include images in your marketing – infographic, *Jeff Bullas*, published 28 May [online] http://www.jeffbullas.com/2012/05/28/ 6-powerful-reasons-why-you-should-include-images-in-your-marketing-infographic/ [accessed 23 February 2016]

'Articles containing relevant images have 94 per cent more total views than articles without images, on average.'

3 Visual content: Kevan Lee (2014) 9 informative infographics to guide your visual content marketing, *Buffer Social*, published 23 July [online] https://blog.bufferapp.com/infographics-visual-content-marketing [accessed 23 February 2016]

'Visual content is 40 times more likely to be shared on social networks.'

4 Smart Phones: (2015) The UK is now a smartphone society, *Ofcom*, published 6 August [online] http://media.ofcom.org.uk/news/2015/cmr-uk-2015/ [accessed 24 February 2016]

'Smartphones have become the hub of our daily lives and are now in the pockets of two thirds (66%) of UK adults.'

5 Sharing Visuals: Travis Balinas (2015) Visual social networks: are Instagram, Pinterest, Snapchat and Vine worth your time? *Outbound Engine,* published 13 October [online] http://www.outboundengine. com/blog/visual-social-networks-are-instagram-pinterest-snapchat-and-vine-worth-your-time/ [accessed 23 February 2016]

'Visual content is a powerful component of social media marketing. Eighty-two per cent of marketers cite images as important or very important to social media content optimization, and 52 per cent believe video content produces the best ROI.'

6 Facebook: Cooper Smith (2013) Facebook users are uploading 350 million new photos each day, *Business Insider*, published 18 September [online] http://www.businessinsider.com/facebook-350-million-photos-each-day-2013-9?IR=T [accessed 24 February 2016]

'Facebook is the world's largest photo-sharing site.'

7 Twitter/Vine: Taylor Casti (2013) The 31 startups Twitter has acquired, *Mashable*, published 18 September [online] http://mashable. com/2013/09/18/twitter-acquisitions/#5asTB7P2zaqx [accessed 23 February 2016]

'October 2012 – In what was certainly its most famous acquisition, Vine, Twitter took a gamble on what the "next big thing" in social media would be – a gamble that seems to have paid off.'

8 Meerkat app: Seth Fiegerman (2015) Meerkat app shows the potential for live streaming on Twitter, *Mashable*, published 2 March [online] http://mashable.com/2015/03/02/meerkat-live-streaming/#cRTsotlN5Eqf [accessed 23 February 2016]

'Many already use Twitter as a platform to broadcast their lives. Now, Meerkat is trying to take that concept to the next level. Meerkat, an app that launched quietly on Friday, gained traction over the weekend… for its effortless approach to turning Twitter into a live streaming platform.'

 9 Periscope: Rhiannon Williams (2015) What is Twitter's new Periscope app? *Telegraph*, published 28 March [online] http://www.telegraph.co.uk/technology/2015/12/010/what-is-twitters-new-periscope-app/ [accessed 23 February 2016]

'Periscope is Twitter's new live-streaming video app, not to be confused with the recently launched Meerkat, also a live-streaming app. It allows you to watch and broadcast live video from all across the globe.'

10 Roman Gubern (2010) *Metamorfosis de la lectura*, Anagrama

11 Katie Stern (2011) *Photo 1: An Introduction to the Art of Photography 1st Edition,* Course Technology, Clifton Park NY

12 Elaine Merieb and Katja Hoehn (2007) *Human Anatomy & Physiology, 7th Edition*, Pearson International Edition, Pearson Longman, London

13 Mobile traffic: Lindsay Kolowich (2015) 25 video marketing statistics for 2015 [Infographic] *Hubspot*, published 10 August [online] http://blog.hubspot.com/marketing/video-marketing-statistics [accessed 23 February 2016]

'Online video now accounts for 50% of all mobile traffic.'

14 Videos online: Michael Brenner (2015) 17 stats that prove 2016 is the year of video, *Marketing Insider Group*, published 8 December [online] http://marketinginsidergroup.com/content-marketing/9818/ [accessed 23 February 2016]

'78% of people watch videos online every week.'

15 Video internet traffic: David Salway (2015) Cisco: video to consume 79% of all internet traffic by 2018, *About Tech*, published 1 October [online] http://broadband.about.com/od/video/fl/Cisco-Video-to-Consume-79-of-all-Internet-Traffic-by-2018.htm [accessed 23 February 2016]

'Cisco predicts that IP video will account for 79 percent of all IP traffic by 2018.'

16 Executive video: (Undated) Video in the C-Suite: Executives embrace the non-text web, *Forbes Insights* [online] http://images.forbes.com/forbesinsights/StudyPDFs/Video_in_the_CSuite.pdf [accessed 23 February 2016]

'Senior executives are also turning to video more frequently. Three-quarters (75%) of executives surveyed said they watch work-related videos on business-related websites at least weekly; more than half (52%) watch work-related videos on YouTube at least weekly.'

17 Executive video: (Undated) Video in the C-Suite: Executives embrace the non-text web: *Forbes Insights* [online] http://images.forbes.com/forbesinsights/StudyPDFs/Video_in_the_CSuite.pdf [accessed 23 February 2016]

'Video is Business Social: Overall, 54% of senior executives share work-related videos with colleagues at least weekly, and almost as many receive work-related [videos] from colleagues.'

18 Ivan Turgenev (1862) *Fathers and Sons*, OUP Oxford (2008)

19 Infographics: John Noble Wilford (2014) Cave Paintings in Indonesia may be among the oldest known, *New York Times*, published 8 October [online] http://www.nytimes.com/2014/10/09/science/ancient-indonesian-find-may-rival-oldest-known-cave-art.html?_r=0 [accessed 24 February 2016]

'The researchers said the earliest images, with a minimum age of 39,900 years, are the oldest known stenciled outlines of human hands in the world.'

20 Punch cartoon: (Undated) About PUNCH magazine, cartoon archive, *Punch* [online] http://www.punch.co.uk/about/ [accessed 23 February 2016]

'Punch, magazine of humour and satire, ran from 1841–2002. A very British institution renowned internationally for its wit and irreverence, it introduced the term "Cartoon" as we know it today and published the works of great comic writers and poets...'

21 Dumb Ways to Die: Metro Trains Melbourne (2012) Dumb Ways to Die, *YouTube*, published 14 November [online] https://www.youtube.com/watch?v=IJNR2EpS0jw [accessed 24 February 2016]

'YouTube 24 February 2016: 122,919,727 views.'

22 Dollar Shave Club: Dollar Shave Club (2012) DollarShaveClub.com – Our Blades Are F***ing Great, *YouTube*, published 6 March [online] https://www.youtube.com/watch?v=ZUG9qYTJMsI [accessed 24 February 2016]

'*YouTube 24 February 2016: 22,017,798 views.*'

23   Nike + Running App: Hannah Becker (2013) Nike+ GPS running app review, *Technology Guide,* published 10 April [online] http://www. technologyguide.com/softwarereview/nike-gps-running-app-review/ [accessed 24 February 2016]

'*Users may also register with the Nike+ website to connect with a community of Nike+ users. The platform allows users to compete against, or train with, friends and strangers alike by syncing and storing running routes, which can later be searched and shared.*'

24   X Factor: John Plunkett (2010) X Factor final peaks at nearly 20 million viewers, *guardian,* published 13 December [online] http://www. theguardian.com/tv-and-radio/2010/dec/13/x-factor-final-record-high [accessed 24 February 2016]

'*Last night's results show averaged 17.2 million viewers, a 55% share of the audience, between 7.30pm and 9.30pm on ITV1. The audience peaked with 19.4 million viewers – a 60% share – between 9.20pm and 9.25pm as Cardle was announced the winner.*'

25   Combined relevance: Dan Zarella (2010) Zombie marketing: how to use combined relevance to go viral, *Dan Zerella The Social Media Scientist,* posted January 14 [online] http://danzarrella.com/zombie-marketing-how-to-use-combined-relevance-to-go-viral/ [accessed 24 February 2016]

'*I asked people why they shared content online, both one-to-one… and broadcast (like Tweeting). In both cases the faraway most common answer was relevance… this seems pretty obvious, but how as a marketer can we capitalize on this? The answer is Combined Relevance.*'

26   Super Bowl: Associated Press (2013) Superdome power outage delays Super Bowl XLVII: *NFL,* published 3 February [online] http://www.nfl. com/superbowl/story/0ap1000000134895/article/superdome-power-outage-delays-super-bowl-xlvii [accessed 24 February 2016]

'*NEW ORLEANS – The Super Bowl turned into Blackout Sunday. The biggest game of the year was halted for 34 minutes because of a power outage, plunging parts of the Superdome into darkness and leaving TV viewers with no football and no explanation why.*'

27 Oreo cookie tweet: Daniel Terdiman (2013) How Oreo's brilliant blackout tweet won the Super Bowl, *cnet.com*, published 4 February [online] http://www.cnet.com/uk/news/how-oreos-brilliant-blackout-tweet-won-the-super-bowl/ [accessed 24 February 2016]

'As… millions waited, Oreo (tweeted) "Power out? No problem,"… along with a hastily put-together image of an ad showing an Oreo and the terrific tag line, "You can still dunk in the dark." The tweet caught fire, and as of this writing had been retweeted 13,734 times.'

The journey from 07 engagement to opportunity

Producing content is a necessary outcome of prospects and customers going online to stay informed, research and make purchasing decisions. Ultimately, websites, blogs and social platforms work as media channels. The currency of media is content. By creating value for potential buyers, salespeople and marketers can encourage prospects to enter the Digital Sales Funnel. Valuable material can then subsequently keep prospects engaged in order to retain their attention. This allows the salesperson or company to earn mindshare. Consequently, when a person is ready to make a purchase, there is every chance that the salesperson or company will be in the prospect's buying set.

This means that content has to create value in relation to what a company offers. A good starting point in achieving this is to think of the challenges that a customer has that might lead them to look for solutions. For example, a recruitment agent might decide that their customers' core challenges are as follows:

How do we find the right candidate?

What do we need to offer in terms of salary and benefits to attract the right person?

How do I avoid making mistakes and know I have the right individual?

What are the best mechanisms for retaining great employees?

If a recruitment agent simply produces material detailing what they do, it will not be engaging. The only people who will possibly interact with the information are those actively looking for a recruitment agent at the time. This would be purely transactional. The recruitment agent would be relying on being found just at the point of purchase. Of course, having undertaken some research first, there may be other agents already in the purchaser's buying set. Moreover, when focusing on 'what' it does, it is unlikely that a recruitment agent could convey much that wouldn't be repeated by many other suppliers. It therefore becomes extremely difficult to differentiate its offering.

Given that the buyer's criteria for purchase are likely to already be defined at the point at which they are merely looking for a supplier, as stated in previous chapters, the recruitment agent will be in a race to the bottom. This means that the agent will be asked to ensure it can meet the prospect's predetermined requirements. Then, with little differentiation and no chance to affect the criteria of purchase, the recruitment agency will be hammered on price.

By creating value around 'what' it delivers, a company can attract prospects into the Digital Sales Funnel much earlier in the purchase journey, or even before a transaction has been considered. Providing value gives the recruitment company the opportunity to earn credibility and trust with the prospect. Consequently, when they are ready to buy, our recruitment agent is in the buying set of the purchaser. There is also the chance that if a prospect finds the material useful, they will share some of it with colleagues. In this way, word of mouth is created and attracts more individuals into the Digital Sales Funnel.

Each challenge that the recruitment agent listed provides a plethora of content that can be produced. For example, challenge number one, 'How do we find the right candidate?', supplies a number of opportunities. A two-minute 'how to' video giving top tips for finding appropriate candidates could be created. Interviewing top HR directors and consultants about how they identify talent in the market could be insightful. Producing downloadable tip sheets with suggestions for finding appropriate staff is another way in which the first identified challenge could be answered.

Similarly, challenge number two, 'What do we need to offer in terms of salary and benefits to attract the right person?', could lead to our recruitment agent producing a market watch newsletter on a quarterly basis. It would detail the current expectations in the market in terms of remuneration. This may be a resource that prospects would find useful and on which they might start to rely. Of course, if and when they required a recruitment agent, it would be very likely that this agency would be in the buying set of the purchaser.

In previous chapters we covered the importance of salespeople and marketers defining exactly 'who' the customer is. We established that this should be defined in as narrow terms as possible, while still being able to meet all the commercial goals on a sensible market share.

Why this is essential is compounded when examining content creation. The wider the audience to whom you are trying to appeal, the necessarily more generic the content becomes. Consequently, it is less useful and not as engaging. Conversely, the narrower the audience, the more relevant the material can be, and this results in it being far more valuable.

For example, we noted that in answer to challenge number two, 'What do we need to offer in terms of salary and benefits to attract the right person?', our recruitment agent could produce a market watch newsletter, on a quarterly basis, detailing current expectation in terms of remuneration. However, if this recruitment agent was trying to appeal to a wide range of industries, positions and even geographical areas, this newsletter might not be possible. With so many variables it could simply take too much research and resource to produce. And even if the recruitment company had the money and personnel to create the newsletter, it would have to be so large that it may put people off from trying to find the data relevant to them. Moreover, it would have to keep the information fairly general in order not to become completely unmanageable.

Let's instead say this recruitment agent specialized in temporary recruitment in the City of Birmingham and it had assessed that the market was big enough to reach all of its commercial objectives on a relatively small market share. This newsletter would now be extremely targeted. It could carry quite detailed information around changes in the market in terms of pay, availability of work and the type of employment being offered, and seasonal variations that may be specific to Birmingham because of the particular sectors that have a strong presence in the area. It could even carry insights and comments from local specialist consultants or HR managers at some of the larger companies that utilize temporary staff. Of course, this newsletter would now be useless to most employers throughout the United Kingdom, but for those businesses utilizing temporary staff in the Birmingham area, it could be invaluable.

Often, poor content is a result of not defining 'who' the customer is in specific enough terms. It then becomes so generic as to be relatively useless. Either that or it simply blends in with the other innumerable pieces of content that are general and bland. This being the case, the content is then likely to fail in attracting any potential buyers to the Digital Sales Funnel.

In order to create material that is valuable to prospects and is therefore effective in attracting them to the Digital Sales Funnel and retaining their attention, it is worth considering using 'buyer personas'. In essence, a buyer persona is a representation of a purchaser that enables a salesperson, or marketing team, to better understand the buyer and the behaviour that results in a buying decision. Content can then be created to reflect this information.

Before a company embarks on utilizing buyer personas it has to establish 'who' the customer is. If this is defined too widely, buying personas become so generic as to be useless and not insightful at all. For example, our recruitment company defined its 'who' as those businesses that use temporary recruitment in Birmingham.

Once the 'who' has been established, there are a number of considerations that have to be deliberated to create a buying persona. All of these should be research based and utilize real evidence. This can be from the actual data that a trading business should have about their different purchasers, and the customer journey on which they embarked. Companies should also speak to customers to better understand their situation and what led them to a particular purchasing decision. Finally, companies will often have to engage in some qualitative research in order to obtain a complete picture.

The first question to ask when creating these buyer personas is, 'What role does the purchaser occupy?' For example, based on its customer data, our recruitment agent might define three different purchasers. These are managing directors at smaller businesses, and HR directors and operations directors at bigger companies. It might be that when identifying the buyer or buyers, companies also want to create buyer personas for the key influencers in the decision. It is the most important personnel in the decision-making process for whom buying personas will be modelled.

Having established the purchaser's role, it is worth identifying some general demographic details about them. For example, their age, gender, marital status, whether they have children, where they live, household income and educational background are all useful kinds of information to acknowledge.

The next consideration is understanding what the buyer is trying to accomplish. In business this would mean taking into account a prospect's responsibilities, the areas of the business on which they are focused, current strategies for achieving those goals and how success is recognized and remunerated. It is important to grasp what goes on within an organization that entices certain individuals to solve an issue, or improve a situation, when so many other prospects settle for the status quo. You would also need to consider a buyer's own professional and personal objectives.

In tandem with this, it is also important to understand the barriers to a purchase. In other words, what are the concerns a purchaser has that might prevent them from ultimately going ahead? These, of course, can be personal, organizational or political, in terms of other key personnel who may have influence over a decision.

Psychographics also need to be examined. These are the values, opinions, attitudes and general lifestyles of these types of individuals. It is often necessary to engage in some qualitative research in order to obtain some valuable insights in this area. Qualitative research can also assist in understanding why purchasers make their buying decisions; having a clearer awareness of the motives behind the conclusions people reach can be invaluable.

Identifying when a prospect actually buys can also be critical. In the Digital Sales Funnel, nurturing prospects by retaining their attention is vital. Therefore, having a greater comprehension of when someone is likely to make a purchase, and perhaps being able to recognize the behaviour they exhibit at this time, can ensure opportunities are pinpointed, capitalized on and certainly don't get missed.

The final consideration is where these potential buyers learn. In other words, where are the places they go to educate themselves and undertake the research to inform their decisions? Not only is this critical information in completing the buyer persona model, but it also affects content distribution.

Obviously, specific items of content will be placed on the different real estate a company or salesperson owns. This can be a website, blog, Facebook page, LinkedIn profile, Twitter account or YouTube channel etc. However, it is critical that you ask the question, 'Where do my customers learn?' For, ultimately, it is in these places that salespeople and marketing departments should ensure they get content placed. Whether this is on industry association sites, active forums, particular blogs or other networks, it is essential that salespeople and companies try to have a presence in the places their customers educate themselves.

Often, the owners of this online real estate will gladly accept content if it is value led and not purely self-promotional. This is because they also possess media channels that require numerous amounts of material to keep customers interested and engaged. Therefore, companies and organizations are often predisposed to taking content that provides value for their audience, as long as it is not a blatant attempt for publicity. Of course, just as authors have always put their name to articles, it is perfectly acceptable to have a credit for the content with a link back to a website, blog or other channel.

Herein lies another key to ensuring that the material a company or salesperson produces leads to sales further down the line. For every piece of content produced, the question should be asked, what do I want my prospect to do next? In other words, having read the article, watched the video or listened to the podcast, what is the call to action to keep the potential purchaser engaged?

Links from content placed on other organizations' websites, or on social media platforms, should always go to a dedicated landing page. A distinct piece of content aimed at a particular audience and which addresses a definite challenge, or a specific context, should not then direct a prospect to a generic page within a website or a general home page. It is more effective to take someone to a page where the key themes can be highlighted, similar language can be used, images can be chosen that are likely to resonate within the exact situation, and relevant calls to action can be suggested.

So, for example, a video could encourage viewers to click a link to receive a free gift. The link may go to a dedicated landing page that repeats the themes of the video with similar visuals being utilized. The free gift may be an e-book providing a series of hints and tips. An e-mail address could be required in order to download the e-book. Thus, data capture is achieved and the prospect enters the Digital Sales Funnel. As well as being encouraged to sign up to a newsletter, a few days later, the individual prospect may be invited to a webinar.

Plotting a customer journey and ensuring there are always calls to action is vital in order to ensure sales are achieved down the line. It is simply absurd that commercial businesses produce content after which there is no obvious way for a prospect to find out more, should that be their inclination. Understanding this journey also enables a company to constantly improve the effectiveness of its activities. For example, maybe people watch the video but do not click on the link. Is the video conveying a powerful enough message? Is the promise of a free gift effective? By asking these questions the company can test, measure and try alternatives to be constantly improving the return it obtains from its sales and marketing efforts.

Ensuring content is placed in the places where prospects learn, creating dedicated landing pages and including compelling calls to action on any material, are all essential aspects of making sure that the efforts salespeople and marketing departments put into their digital activities reap rewards. Ultimately, salespeople and marketers have to concentrate their efforts on specific groups and provide value in order to engage them. This journey can sometimes occur over quite an extensive period of time.

Regular engagement results in earning the mindshare of a target audience. Thus, when they are ready to make a purchase, it is likely that the salesperson or marketing team that has this attention will be in the prospect's buying set. Being able to engage prospects with a degree of regularity is vital to making the Digital Sales Funnel work.

While it is clear that the most important aspect of engagement is ensuring prospects receive value at all times, salespeople and marketing teams are able to use content to move people along the buying journey. One of the keys to both engaging individuals and guiding them towards a purchase is the use of narrative.

Telling stories is the best way to teach, persuade, and obtain and keep people's attention. Today, salespeople and marketing teams own media channels. Their effectiveness is predicated on stories. When we speak to each other we tend to talk in stories. We use them as a mechanism to explain how our day was, to convey our hopes and ambitions, to provide the reasons for our likes and dislikes or to describe particular experiences.

The biggest-selling book of all time is the Bible.[1] It contains some of the greatest narratives in history. Despite the fact that we are extremely familiar with these stories, they still have the ability to capture our imagination. We just have to look at the plethora of films that even today are being produced based on biblical tales.[2] For example, in 2014 alone, two huge blockbuster movies, Noah and Exodus: Gods and Kings, were both released.[3]

We remember stories in a way that we don't with data, facts and figures. This is because stories humanize a message, and make it something to which we can immediately relate. That is why parables, which can be traced back to the Bible, and fables, normally associated with Aesop, a slave in Ancient Greece,[4] are such powerful mechanisms for communicating a moral message. One could simply list a code of ethical conduct, which might make perfect sense on a logical level. However, the effectiveness of stories is that they don't just deliver a logical message but move us emotionally.

The fact is, if you want to get someone to act, you need to stir them emotionally. We know from neuroscience that emotions play a vital role in decision making. In his 1994 book *Descartes' Error: Emotion, reason and the human brain*, Antonio Damasio makes the suggestion that emotion is fundamental in making decisions when dealing with equal options. In other words, when operating in a market where differentiation is difficult, the experience you provide, and therefore how you make someone feel, will most likely create the competitive advantage.

In his book, Damasio demonstrated how people with prefrontal cortical damage to the brain were unable to make effective decisions. These people were seemingly normal, except that they were unable to feel emotions, and due to this, they could not decide preferences. For example, the book contains the story of Elliot who, having no emotion, could not even decide which colour socks to wear.

In business-to-consumer communications, there are plenty of examples of emotional messaging, but in the business-to-business world, marketers and salespeople tend to concentrate on the logical benefits and reasons for purchasing their offer. However, human nature does not change just because someone is operating in a corporate environment, so it is vital to reach people emotionally as well as addressing them on a logical level.

The combination of owning media channels which thrive on stories, together with the requirement to touch people emotionally, makes narrative absolutely essential for every marketer and salesperson. Being able to deliver insights within the context of a story is much more likely to resonate with a prospect, and to influence their thinking.

Of course, the narrative should tie directly back to where the company proposition outperforms competitors, the organization has some advantages, or areas where the offering is particularly compelling. Stories, however, don't have to give solutions. Sometimes a powerful narrative that simply demonstrates the cost of failing to act, can be an extremely potent way of getting a prospect to think. Of course, there is an implication that the protagonist of the tale has the answers. This can be reinforced with the subsequent calls to action that are made available.

The importance of narrative cannot be underestimated in a media setting. The ability of stories to touch people and encourage them to act makes their use invaluable. Of course, the other aspect of touching people emotionally is through the 'social' side of social media. What makes digital channels different from traditional media is the ability of the audience to respond. Conventional publishing, cinema, radio and television are, in the main, one-way traffic. Usually, content is created by the publisher or broadcaster and then received by the audience. On digital channels, everyone can reply.

Of course, it is this interaction that makes the medium so powerful. In this environment, therefore, there are certain principles which should be a guide to ensure that the 'social' side of social media is utilized well.

First, it is essential that both salespeople and companies are authentic. Trying to be something they are not is likely to be found out over time, and then all trust and credibility will be lost. Moreover, people connect with an individual's humanity. It is being themselves, and being genuine, that makes the interaction with them different from anyone else. Listening is also vital. When face to face, no one would throw a barrage of thoughts or ideas at another human being and leave the room before they had the chance to reply. If a response was given, it would most likely elicit a further reaction. This, of course, is referred to as a conversation. Yet online there are people who will post their thoughts and opinions and not acknowledge any response they may receive. This is as rude in an online environment as it would be offline. Digital is a two-way medium, so you should expect to receive comments from the content you post and also make sure you respond.

Listening is also key to ensuring that the material that salespeople and marketers produce is relevant. Monitoring conversations, social media posts and dialogue in forums etc., will provide sales-people and marketers with real-time insights. Consequently, it enables them to discern the hot topics, issues and challenges people are interested in.

Monitoring and observing are also part of the way to understand the rules and culture of any particular online community. Whether it is a social platform, an online forum or another network, every community will have variations on acceptable behaviour and do's and don'ts. It is very important when participating in these different groups to observe the protocols that are expected in order not to offend other participants.

Of course, the reason why salespeople and marketers will be engaging on these digital platforms is ultimately to win business. However, these channels are two-way, and it is vital to give as well as to take. People must be willing to share content that resonates and might be useful to connections in their network. Salespeople and marketers should be willing to 'like' something on Facebook, retweet it on Twitter, +1 it on Google+, and endorse their fellow professionals they would be happy to recommend on LinkedIn. These activities are reciprocal and people will be less inclined to share a person's content and expertise if they seem unwilling to do the same. Similarly, they should ensure they thank and acknowledge those people who do share their material and publicly endorse it in some way.

Endnotes

1 Bible: (undated) Best-selling book of non-fiction, *Guinness World Records* [online] http://www.guinnessworldrecords.com/world-records/best-selling-book-of-non-fiction [accessed 24 February 2016]

'Although it is impossible to obtain exact figures, there is little doubt that the Bible is the world's best-selling... book. A survey by the Bible Society concluded that around 2.5 billion copies were printed between 1815 and 1975, but more recent estimates put the number at more than 5 billion.'

2 Bible movies 2014: (undated) List of films based on the Bible, *Wikipedia* [online] https://en.wikipedia.org/wiki/List_of_films_based_on_the_Bible [accessed 24 February 2016]

This Wikipedia page lists 89 movies based on the Hebrew Bible alone.

3 Bible movies 2014: (undated) List of films based on the Bible: *Wikipedia* [online] https://en.wikipedia.org/wiki/List_of_films_based_on_the_Bible [accessed 24 February 2016]

'The Flood – Genesis 6–9: Noah (2014)... Moses and Israel in the desert: Exodus: Gods and Kings (2014).'

4 Aesop's Fables: John Horgan (2014) Aesop's Fables, *Ancient History Encyclopedia*, published 8 March [online] http://www.ancient.eu/article/664/ [accessed 24 February 2016]

'Written by a former Greek slave, in the late- to mid-6th century BCE, Aesop's Fables are the world's best-known collection of morality tales. These stories... often portraying animals or insects representing humans engaged in human-like situations... Ultimately represent one of the oldest characteristics of human life: storytelling.'

Getting noticed 08

I was once invited to speak to a board at a fairly large public limited company (plc). They had asked me to come and explain how customer behaviour was changing, and what the implications were for their sales and marketing activities. Having given my presentation, we then entered into a question and answer session.

Arms folded, a rather cautious member of the board made the following observation. They conceded that once there is a community in place, momentum could be built and so there was a possibility that prospects could be engaged through the value that the plc created. They also noted that if only a small minority of prospects shared material it would, nevertheless, attract more people into the Digital Sales Funnel in the most credible way, that is, by recommendation. However, the problem this board member identified was where to begin. How do you build a community or create an audience out of nothing?

While, on the surface, this seemed like a fair question, I found it rather perplexing. This plc already had a potential audience, because it currently had people buying its products and services. I asked this particular member of the board approximately how many customers the company currently served. The immediate response was around 4,000. So what would happen, I asked, if we searched for those individual purchasers, and their businesses, and started following them on Twitter, Facebook, LinkedIn, Google+, etc? Would some follow us back? If we provided them with content that they found valuable, would any be likely to engage? Could we start to build an audience that way? Of course, the answer was a resounding 'yes'.

While the initial contact base will be much smaller, even a start-up business, or salesperson, in a brand new sector or industry will have some people with whom they can start to interact. Whether it is relevant friends, colleagues, ex-school or university contacts, partners, suppliers, or existing customers, there will be people who can be approached, even when you are just starting out. Of course, in this way, salespeople, marketers and companies have the opportunity to begin establishing a Digital Sales Funnel of their own.

Creating value is the key means by which prospects can be attracted into the Digital Sales Funnel. Ultimately, potential buyers will only interact with a salesperson, or organization, if they are obtaining something for their time, and with so much information and content online, it is clearly not enough to merely provide value and hope that it is discovered. Ensuring the material that salespeople and companies develop gets noticed is vital in being able to attract prospects into the top of the Digital Sales Funnel.

Apart from leveraging existing contacts, there are other methods for building the Digital Sales Funnel from a standing start. Essentially, with regards to prospecting and lead generation, what a salesperson or marketing team is trying to achieve is to build a community around their business. By community, we are referring to those potential buyers who are regularly 'engaging' with a salesperson, or company, through the value that they are providing.

Of course, these communities already exist. There will be other businesses and organizations that currently serve a particular group of people who might represent part, or all, of the audience a salesperson or company wants to address. Therefore, partnering with these entities becomes an extremely efficient way of reaching a specific target market.

There are a variety of reasons why an organization would be willing to partner with another business. First, if both have a similar target audience, with comparable numbers already engaged, then each has the opportunity to attract more prospects into its Digital Sales Funnel in a credible way.

For example, an IT maintenance company and a security software provider each serve medium-size businesses in the south east of England. Both have around 1,000 customers. Together, they decided to create a series of tip sheets and short videos for their clientele, who are the IT directors and IT managers at the companies they supply. In so doing, there are three excellent outcomes.

First, by sharing the costs of the videos and tip sheets, the two businesses create content with less expense, both in terms of time and money, than either could have achieved on their own. Second, together they provide value that neither could have produced as individual entities. The IT maintenance provider has insight around cloud computing, servers, hardware and network infrastructure that the security firm does not possess. Similarly, the security company can impart knowledge around the latest 'must haves' in keeping an organization safe that the IT maintenance provider does not cover. Creating material together makes it more comprehensive, informative and engaging than would have otherwise been the case.

Finally, there may be some small overlap between these respective firms' clientele, but by sharing the content with their customers, including links to dedicated landing pages, each one has the opportunity of reaching approximately 1,000 potential new prospects in a very credible way. After all, each business is partnering with a trusted supplier as far as the recipient of the content is concerned. Of course, in this scenario, some potential purchasers may very well be encouraged to enter the Digital Sales Funnel of the organization they have just become aware of.

Therefore, successful partnerships achieve two main outcomes. First, they further engagement with existing prospects by supplying them with value that an organization could not create on its own. Second, exposure to the partner company's audience enables a business to reach a whole new set of prospects in a credible way.

Even when an individual salesperson or company does not have a prospect base or clientele as large as a potential partner, it does not preclude the two working together. It can be that a potential partner values the content creation more than the size of the audience. Consequently, a large business may be willing to collaborate with a smaller entity in order to receive content of value with which it can engage its readers. In order for a partnership to work effectively, the main aspect should be that both are addressing a similar audience with complimentary offerings. That being the case, by working together, new value can be created for customers.

Of course, it is not just partnerships that can provide the opportunity for a salesperson or business to reach new prospects. Engaging with influencers is another way of accessing a target audience. An influencer is someone whose opinions and recommendations will affect the actions, choices and behaviours of others. In any given market sector, subject area, and within a geographical location, there will be influencers. These are people with significantly more reach and resonance than the average person.

By reach, we literally mean, to how many people is a message communicated? For example, an individual on Twitter may have a million followers, and so potentially this person would have a lot of reach. However, while reach is certainly a factor in measuring influence, it is not enough. As well as reach, you must also possess resonance. In terms of resonance, the key question to ask is, 'Does anyone care about the messages a person conveys?'

In other words, our individual on Twitter, with a million followers, may send out a link encouraging all of them to watch 'the funniest clip of the year'. If 20 people were to click on the link, it would suggest that while this person has reach, they have no resonance. Basically, no one seems to care what they think. On the other hand, if 800,000 people were to click on the link, it would suggest that not only does this person have reach, but they also have a great deal of resonance amongst their audience. It would seem that people take their recommendations particularly seriously.

Offline, it is almost impossible to have reach without resonance. In the main, reach comes from a person's message being carried by traditional broadcasting and publishing channels. These media companies will only carry a message because they think that their audience is interested in what the individual has to say. In other words, reach is an outcome of resonance. So, if the president of the United States makes a statement on the security of the nation, because they have resonance, they obtain reach by virtue of their message being carried by so much of the media.

Online this is not necessarily the case. It is possible for individuals to appear to have reach but have no resonance whatsoever. This could be because a person has paid for followers and so their apparent reach is not real. Alternatively, it could be because they were once 'flavour of the month' but people then lost interest without unsubscribing or unfollowing them in great numbers. Ultimately, an influencer is someone with both reach and resonance.

Whether it is a salesperson working in a new territory, or a business venturing into different market places, it is worth investigating who the influencers are in a particular sector or area. Amongst others, influencers could be bloggers, vloggers, business analysts, heads of communities, captains of industry, company leaders, commentators, recognized experts or people holding prominent positions. Identifying the influencers enables salespeople and marketing teams to undertake a variety of activities.

As with partners, working with influencers can be incredibly beneficial. Having them write a guest post, interviewing them for a video or podcast, or conversely contributing content on their platforms, can put a salesperson or business in front of a large number of people in a very credible way.

Even when it is not possible to work directly with influencers, they can still be leveraged. It is often worth informing them of a new service or even sending them a product to review. For example, I once worked with a manufacturer of musical instruments who sent out a new product to a variety of influencers. The product was sent as a gift with no obligation on the influencers whatsoever. However, reputation plays an essential role in the influence people accumulate. These people are normally considered 'in the know' by their followers. Therefore, reviewing a new model of musical instrument, before it was available to purchase, would make these influencers look good and enhance their reputations. This being the case, the company was sure that it would receive some reviews.

Of course, the company was worried. What if the instrument got panned? What if the influencers didn't like the product? To which the obvious answer was, don't make bad equipment. In other words, if this instrument was universally perceived to be poor, then, in an age of social media and digital, where everyone has a channel, it would most likely be doomed in any case. Of course, receiving good reviews, which was indeed the outcome in this instance, enabled this music manufacturer to achieve a high level of demand in the market, even before the instrument went on general sale.

It is possible to pay influencers in order for them to feature a particular product or service in a video or blog. If this is the case, it must be made known to the audience that the influencer is receiving a remuneration. It must not be done surreptitiously. Apart from being unscrupulous and unethical, it also violates guidelines in many countries and is against the law in several others.[1]

Of course, in many ways, once an organization pays an influencer, they are veering into the realms of 'endorsements' and 'sponsorships'. In the offline world, sponsorships used to be for the rich and famous. After all, they were the only individuals to have resonance and, therefore, reach. Consequently, it was an expensive mechanism and so tended to be a tactic used by very large organizations. Today, this is not the case. Within small niche markets there will be influencers who, while widely followed and respected within an industry, are not famous outside of their specialism. However, in an age where these people own their own channels, their 'influence' can be extremely valuable, so it is often worth leveraging.

Identifying where the influencers in any particular market are active can also be incredibly useful. We have stated that content cannot solely be posted on a salesperson's or company's real estate, for example a website, blog, Facebook, Instagram, YouTube or Twitter account. A key question for any salesperson or marketing team to ask is, 'Where do my customers learn?' Salespeople and marketers need to try to have a presence on the platforms that are used by their potential buyers.

To this end, it can be very informative to observe where influencers post and communicate. After all, if these are people with the most reach and resonance in their market, then there is a good chance that the places where they post content are pertinent platforms where you should have a presence. Therefore, aside from their own channels, it is worth noting the forums, blogs, websites, networks and social media platforms in which particular influencers participate. It may well be worthwhile for a salesperson or business to invest time in some of these destinations.

Finally, influencers can be a good source of ideas. Bearing in mind that these individuals are the ones most followed and listened to by a specific audience, one would expect the topics about which they write or speak to be particularly germane. Following the subjects covered by influencers can often provide salespeople and marketing teams with ideas for their own material. It may very well be that a company or individual has a distinctive view on an area of discussion covered by an influencer. As a way of forging new material, influencers can often provide inspiration that enables people to develop their own content.

Leveraging partnerships and influencers is a key way for a sales-person or company to increase their own credibility and attain some awareness amongst an audience. Another method for achieving this is developing a 'round robin' article.

We inhabit a world today where everyone owns online channels, which are incredibly content hungry. It takes a lot of material to keep a platform vibrant and interesting. This is especially true for those businesses that publish online magazines, whether a printed version exists or not, or operate web portals for a particular industry. These companies want visitors to regularly engage with their site, but people will only be encouraged to keep coming back to a portal if it contains fresh content each time they visit.

In this scenario, publishing companies are often predisposed to taking good material from all sorts of sources so long as it has value for their audience. An article that addresses a pertinent issue, and that quotes industry leaders, is potentially a really interesting piece of content. This is essentially what a 'round robin' article achieves.

For example, an organization that offers leadership mentoring and training approached a well-known publisher that produces an online portal and magazine aimed at the human resources (HR) community. HR personnel are key buyers of this company's services. They explained to the editor at the publishing house that they were writing an extensive article on the effectiveness of the mentoring and training support that leaders receive in organizations today, and its perceived importance in the performance of a business. They told the editor that they would be interviewing some of the UK's leading HR directors at a few of the UK's most successful companies. Of course, the editor agreed to take the article.

The organization then approached a number of leading HR directors, at some of the UK's biggest companies, asking if they were willing to undertake a 10- to 15-minute interview to be featured in an article for this magazine and portal. The aforementioned magazine is very well known as it is widely read by a large percentage of those working in HR positions in the UK. Therefore, while not everyone agreed, many were quite willing to be questioned for the prestigious title.

Immediately this enabled the salesperson at the leadership mentoring and training company to have conversations with some of the foremost HR directors in the UK. In an ideal world, all of the interviews would have been carried out face to face, but some were undertaken on the phone. Nevertheless, it allowed the salesperson to have an interesting and insightful conversation with some potentially fantastic prospects, in the most credible way.

Once the article was written, and posted on the HR portal, the salesperson sent the link to all the participants, thanking them for their time and highlighting their contribution to the piece. This enabled the salesperson to start to solidify the relationships created, and earn credibility and trust with potential buyers who they may have struggled to get in front of in any other way. Over time, a couple of these HR directors did indeed become customers.

Moreover, the credibility the salesperson earned by having an article on such a well-known website was enormous. From their blog to other social media, they wrote about different aspects of the article with links back to the main body of work on the portal. They referred to it in conversations with other prospects. It was a great way of getting in front of some fantastic new potential customers, creating a brilliant piece of content, earning credibility and trust, and building some awareness in the sector.

Another way the salesperson utilized this 'round robin' article, and a more general technique in helping individuals to get noticed, is 'tagging'. Online, 'tagging' has a variety of connotations. In terms of social media, what we mean by 'tagging' is adding a person's name to a piece of content when it is posted. In so doing this creates a link to their profile as well as notifying them that they have been 'tagged'.

For the salesperson, 'tagging' the people they interviewed had a number of benefits. First, people seeing the post may have recognized some of the well-known individuals that had been 'tagged'. This can make a post seem more authoritative and appealing, and might have encouraged certain individuals who may have otherwise ignored the article to take a closer look at the material.

Second, notifying the interviewees they had been 'tagged' in a post in which they were featured, encouraged some to share the material with their networks. After all, these HR directors were being quoted in a substantial article on a well-known industry portal. It made them look good, so why not share it with colleagues? By tagging these people the salesperson had a chance of obtaining greater reach for their content, which is exactly what occurred.

Tagging should not be overused or employed inappropriately. For example, tagging someone in a post because they are well known, when the material has nothing to do with them, is exploitative. Apart from the fact they can untag themselves, the perpetrator could be reported, depending on the platform. Similarly, constantly tagging the same individuals, even when something might be relevant, could result in the loss of any goodwill that did exist. At best the protagonist may simply be ignored, at worst it could lead to complaints. However, used in the right way, tagging can be a great way of engaging someone and obtaining greater exposure for content.

Tagging is not the only way to use others in order to get noticed. Done sparingly, you can ask connections for introductions to people. On many social platforms, it is possible to see who is in a friend's or colleague's network. If there is someone to whom an introduction would be pertinent, asking to be introduced can be a great way of initiating a conversation.

When requesting an introduction you should try to create a compelling reason to become acquainted, rather than merely wanting to connect, or worse still, 'sell' to someone. For example, you might suggest you want to interview an individual for an article or podcast. Of course, personal introductions have always been better than cold approaches, but creating a context for the approach that is interesting for the recipient and not just the salesperson, makes it more likely that the connection will be well received and is successful over time.

Ultimately, social platforms provide a way of being able to identify those individuals with whom you have someone in common, providing opportunities to utilize networks that were not possible in a previous era.

The power of these networks is the reason why salespeople should get into the habit of connecting with everyone they meet online. For example, having encountered an individual at an exhibition, dropping the person a quick note with an invitation to connect on LinkedIn is a great way of staying in touch. After all, the details in someone's personal contact list don't change automatically when they move jobs or are promoted. However, people do update their social media profiles, and so connecting on social platforms makes it easier to stay in touch with people and be aware of any changes in jobs or roles that may occur.

This level of transparency that now exists because of social platforms means managing reputation is more important than ever before. To this end, salespeople should ensure that as a matter of process, every satisfied customer is asked to post a testimonial on Facebook, Twitter or LinkedIn etc. Although receiving an e-mail extolling the virtues of your offering is very gratifying, it is not particularly helpful. Gone are the days when salespeople walked around with written testimonials, kept in a presentation binder, to show to prospects in meetings.

Today, those references need to be in public places, as people will go online in order to scrutinize a possible supplier long before they get anywhere near their office. Of course, many happy clients will still refrain from posting any positive comments on public platforms, even when asked. However, if salespeople make it part of their procedure to always request a testimonial from every customer, it will have a cumulative effect. Even if relatively few customers comply, over weeks, months and years these testimonials will accrue and enhance the salesperson's reputation.

Asking for testimonials is not the only way of involving customers and prospects in your online activities. Whether it is encouraging comments on a blog, enticing people to contribute their own ideas, posing questions to the community, hosting competitions, or allowing individuals to score material, for example like Amazon's five-star rating mechanism, user-generated content can be extremely beneficial in keeping a platform vibrant and interesting. The more potential purchasers get involved and engage with the material supplied, the better the likelihood of them sharing it with their networks and engaging over the long term.

Whether the content is user generated or not, social sharing is an essential way of reaching new prospects and encouraging more people into the Digital Sales Funnel. With that in mind, it is important to ensure that on any blog, website or platform the 'social sharing' buttons are clearly noticeable and accessible. Failure to encourage people to 'like' something on Facebook, 'share it' on LinkedIn, '+1' it on Google+ or 'tweet' it on Twitter could result in lost opportunities.

With this in mind, it is worth paying attention to the timing of so-cial media posts. In order to make the Digital Sales Funnel as ef-fective as possible, it is important to test and measure every aspect of your activities. For different communities there will be certain times when a post is more likely to get seen and shared. Observing the stats and finding the best moments to provide new material to a particular community is worthwhile when trying to achieve maximum impact with any content that is created.

These timings will also vary depending on the platform itself. For example, you might observe that the best occasions to post to a par-ticular audience on Facebook are on a Thursday or Friday afternoon. On the other hand, the same community might respond better on LinkedIn on a Tuesday morning. Knowing these metrics and con-stantly testing them will help in maximizing impact.

Keywords also play an important part in creating impact with con-tent. One of the major ways to be found is to be seen when someone searches on a particular topic. Without using some of the right keywords or phrases it is unlikely that a website or blog will be discovered.

There are two principle areas to understand when it comes to key-words. The first is traffic. Traffic refers to the number of people searching on a particular keyword each day. Of course, if you are an accountant, and there are tens of thousands of searches for account-ants every day, then in theory, ensuring the keyword 'accountant' is used in content makes sense.

However, the other aspect to keywords is competition. That is, how many other sites and platforms are trying to rank highly for a particular keyword. It is hard to rank highly for a keyword where there is lots of competition. Often, there will be businesses that have already established a firm ranking. This being the case, it is not al-ways the best strategy to try to rank for keywords simply because they receive an abundance of traffic.

Short-tail keywords are those that are one to three words long, but sometimes it is better to try to rank for a longer, more specific phrase. So, rather than the word 'accountant', a firm may try to rank for 'small business accountant in York'. These 'long-tail keywords or phrases', as they are known, are easier to rank for because there are fewer companies trying to optimize content for these distinct phrases rather than the very popular, more generic terms. Although these phrases will attract less traffic, because it is easier for a company to rank well for them, they can still generate good numbers to a website or blog. Whether 'short tail' or 'long tail', any word or phrase that is searched for in significant numbers is considered a keyword.

Researching keywords is not easy. For 'long-tail' phrases, it is worth thinking about words that are relevant to both the business and the target audience. There are companies that will identify keywords, as well as software that will assist in finding them. For more about this software, see Chapter 9.

Of course, like so many other aspects of digital, testing and measuring the effectiveness of different words and phrases is vital. In this way, it is possible for salespeople and companies to utilize the terms that are most potent in ensuring their content is found.

Having identified keywords that work, it is important that the creators of content don't simply undertake 'keyword stuffing'. This is trying to load content with the right keywords as many times as possible within an article. Ultimately, content has to provide value for the audience, so it will be shared and individuals will engage and come back for more. It is unlikely that creating content where there is an aim to continually use certain words or phrases will provide as much value as material where the choice words are used more sparingly and appropriately. Moreover, as search engines have become increasingly sophisticated, they will penalize blatant 'keyword stuffing'. It is, however, useful to use the keyword or phrase in the title of the content if possible.

While the use of keywords within content will assist the chances of being found in organic search, it is also important for marketing departments and salespeople to be aware of the paid alternatives. There will certainly be occasions where paying to receive some attention, in order to enable a business to attract prospects into the top of its Digital Sales Funnel, could certainly be appropriate.

It is important to note that, while a salesperson or marketing department may opt to pay for some attention, they must still provide the audience with value in order to engage them. After all, while the purpose of paying is to enable a business to cut through the noise and get noticed, once this has been achieved, people will still only engage with an individual or company if they receive value for their time.

One of the ways to increase the likelihood of providing value when paying for attention is to think seriously about context. In other words, what are the events taking place that would make it likely a prospect would respond to the paid efforts of a business? Making promotions contextually relevant will increase their effectiveness.

Amongst the paid methods available are:

Pay-per-click advertising/adwords – Google Adwords and Bing Ads are auction-based platforms. These platforms can deliver highly targeted traffic within a short period of time. Bidding for ad placements can become quite costly and so companies have to work out how much they can afford to pay for acquiring a prospect. Daily, weekly and monthly budgets can be set, putting businesses very much in control, and can be changed on a daily basis. The keywords used to attract the traffic are very important in obtaining the right type of prospects.

Digital display advertising – This works by placing advertising on the blogs, websites, forums and other platforms that are used by prospects. Advertising can take the form of text, images, audio and video etc. Measurements and payments are usually based on cost per thousand impressions (CPM).

Site retargeting – This allows adverts to be shown to prospects after they visit a site. These can be used to encourage prospects to revisit a website. Capping the frequency of retargeting is a good idea to ensure that prospects do not become irritated by the promotions. Retargeting can take other forms. For example, search retargeting is where a user of a search engine can receive display ads based on their search queries.

Social media advertising – There are many social platforms that can be used to drive traffic and leads. Amongst others, Facebook, Instagram, LinkedIn and Twitter have targeting tools that allow companies to address a particular market based on a variety of criteria.

Promoted posts on social media – Facebook allows posts to be promoted, or boosted, as does LinkedIn via its sponsored updates. In both cases the idea is to allow a company's content to be seen by more of its target audience. Whether it is promoted tweets on Twitter or pins on Pinterest, most platforms offer ways of paying in order to increase the number of people who see the content that is published.

Paid content discovery – 'Related articles', with a click through, sit within the page of a website someone is visiting. It allows businesses to promote their content to audiences who may be interested due to the material they are already looking at. Amongst platforms that facilitate this paid content discovery are Taboola and Outbrain.

Video promotion – Online video ads can be overlaid on top of videos or run prior to actual videos. YouTube has perhaps been the most well-known platform for this type of promotion, although Facebook, amongst others, now has its own video options.

Endnote

1 Influencer remuneration: (undated) The Federal Trade Commission 16 CFR Part 255, *ftc.gov*, [online] https://www.ftc.gov/sites/default/files/attachments/press-releases/ftc-publishes-final-guides-governing-endorsements-testimonials/091005revisedendorsementguides.pdf [accessed 9 March 2016]

Author writes: In this document, the FTC states that it can fine the blogger and/or a company for not disclosing an arrangement whereby the company compensates the writer for a positive review.

Tools and platforms 09

Although many of the social networks operate in different ways, to a greater or lesser extent, all provide the opportunity to contribute information that creates a profile. When completing this portrait, there are certain aspects that people should keep in mind.

Photo – A good professional photograph is important if you want people to take you seriously. In the main, a favourable head shot should be used to convey the right impression.

Overview/bio – Individuals should ensure they create an outline of themselves that is not too long and is interesting to read. Think about the information and experience that will be significant to others. What facts will assist in communicating credibility, knowledge and expertise?

Other information – Where social platforms encourage additional details to be added, such as education, experiences, awards, interests etc., you should include as many relevant facts as possible. Always keep in mind what would be of interest to customers and prospects. Similarly, where there is the option to upload documents, photos, and embed links, videos and other presentations, it is worth utilizing this opportunity when you have material that will provide value for prospects and customers.

Keywords – It is important to think about the phrases and descriptions you would want to show up if people conduct a search. There are two search functions for which you need to optimize. First, there is the search tool within the social network itself, and second, there is Google. In order to see what a social profile looks like on Google, log out of the particular social platform and then search in Google. The information Google grabs is different depending on the channel. You will be able to see the material Google has used from a public profile, and alter it accordingly. The internal search function for each social platform works differently depending on the network. Instructions on how to optimize for search on the various channels can be found online. As a rule, if it is possible to put the main keyword in the profile or page name, it will help it rank best in both Google searches and within the network itself. Ultimately, however, you must ensure this does not dilute your personal brand, and so it is not a technique that everyone will be able to utilize.

Testimonials – Whether it is a recommendation on LinkedIn or a visitor post on a Facebook page, it is important for salespeople to encourage satisfied customers to leave positive comments on social networks. Gone are the days when salespeople walked around with a folder of letters to show prospects and customers. Today, these endorsements need to be in the public forums where people look.

Platforms and networks

Ultimately, you must think about all this information in terms of how you want to be perceived by prospects and customers. Of course, how you come across is incredibly important to the success you will have in encouraging connections and establishing relationships online.

When utilizing these platforms there are a few areas worth noting. First, connect with everyone. This includes friends and professional associates, past and current co-workers, suppliers, partners, prospects and customers. You should also connect with all the people encountered during the course of business.

When possible, invitations should be personalized. Lots of networks provide standard requests to connect, but they are more likely to be well received if they are directly addressed to the recipient. Social networks have become the best live customer relationship management systems in the world. It is unlikely that a prospect will directly inform a salesperson of a job move or promotion. However, because most will update their details on the social platforms they use, it is easier for salespeople to stay informed about the movements of prospects and customers and their changing roles. In this way, it is possible to keep in touch with them.

Moreover, the larger the audience with whom you are connected, the greater the reach of the posted content and messages. Not only does this material extend to additional direct contacts, but also a bigger number of connections means that there is an increased chance of information being shared with a wider audience.

For example, if 5 per cent of a network shares a certain article, then 5 per cent of 1,000 connections is more than 5 per cent of 200 connections. Furthermore, on an occasion when you want to try to gain an introduction to a particular individual, the bigger your network the more likely that this can be facilitated. Where appropriate, and when there is a compelling reason, it is perfectly acceptable to ask people in your network to be introduced to someone with whom they are connected. Of course, the larger the network the more options there are available.

It is also important to stay active on the networks you choose to utilize. Ultimately, these platforms are media channels. Therefore, they are only as good as the interactions that take place and the content that is posted on them. In the same way as it is the programmes on a TV station, or the stories in a magazine, that make the channel compelling, it is the activity conducted, and the content uploaded, that makes a profile on a social media platform interesting. A lack of vivacity will make a profile seem dull and will mean people are less likely to engage.

Finally, there are platforms such as LinkedIn that offer upgrades and premium accounts. These provide advanced features for a fee. Capabilities such as greater search functionality and more information, for example detailing those individuals who have looked at your profile, can be extremely useful. Other features, such as opportunities to save searches and receive alerts and notifications, mean that paying for the extra facilities is well worth the money when you are utilizing these networks for their commercial pursuits.

There are a multitude of platforms available to a salesperson or marketing team. Of course, no one has the time and resource to be on them all. Ultimately, salespeople and marketing departments should be on the social media sites their customers appropriate. By searching and finding their customers online and, when in conversation, asking them for the sites they use the most, it should be possible for salespeople to keep on top of a few of the networks that are most popular with their prospects and clientele.

While it is impossible to detail every social platform available, below are some of the largest networks that salespeople and marketing departments will want to consider, depending on their client base:

Facebook is the biggest social network in the world, with more active users than any other platform.[1] As well as a personal profile, it is worth operating a company page. Being such a big site, with so many users, it is difficult for almost any company to ignore Facebook right now. This is because it is very likely that a lot of its customers will be on the platform. Facebook Messenger is also currently the world's second most popular messaging app.[2]

WhatsApp is the world's most popular instant messaging provider.[3] Users are not limited to text and can also send photos, videos and voice messages to each other. In October 2014 Facebook acquired WhatsApp.[4]

Tumblr is a microblogging platform and social networking site. It is particularly good for sharing visual content such as photos, memes and GIFs.

Instagram is the most popular photo-sharing site in the world.[5] Short videos can also be shared and it is becoming increasingly prominent with advertisers. Facebook bought Instagram in April 2012.[6]

Twitter is known as a real-time microblogging platform where users' messages are limited to 140 characters. Users are also able to share images and video on the platform. Its ability to disseminate information quickly, to large audiences, is perhaps the reason it became influential.

Snapchat is a mobile-only instant messaging app. Photos and short videos can be sent which automatically disappear a few seconds after they have been viewed. The 'stories' feature allows users to share aspects of their day with others. 'Stories' are automatically deleted after 24 hours.

VK – originally VKontakte – is the largest European social networking platform.[7] Although it is available in English, it is really the

Russian version of Facebook and is particularly popular amongst Russian speakers.

Pinterest is a photo-sharing site that, by creating pin boards, allows users to share images, ideas, favourite products and things that they find inspiring. With buy buttons on the pictures of products sold by some retailers, it has a significant influence on many consumer purchases.

LinkedIn is a business-focused professional network. The easily accessible data about its members makes it a very valuable business tool. As well as making connections with individuals, the platform has many very focused business interest groups in which participation can be valuable.

Google+ is backed by the power of the world's largest search engine,[8] and is therefore a platform that should not be ignored. When it originally launched, it also introduced some very useful features, for example Google Hangouts, which now also has its own site.

Flickr is an image- and video-hosting website. With its mobile app it is easy to use from a mobile device.

Vine is a video-sharing service where users can share six-second looping video clips. Twitter acquired Vine in October 2012 before its official launch.[9] Users can share videos on Vine's social platform as well as on networks such as Facebook and Twitter.

Meetup is a social networking platform that enables individuals to organize offline group meetings all over the world. Meet ups are arranged around a wide variety of issues, hobbies and interests.

YouTube is the premier video-sharing site.[10] After Google, YouTube is the world's second-largest search engine.[11] Although Google bought YouTube in November 2006,[12] it still maintains its own identity.

Reddit works like an online bulletin board where users post stories and news via submitted links.

Periscope is a live video-streaming app. Broadcasts can be made viewable to specific users or can be publicly available. Twitter acquired Periscope at the beginning of 2015.[13] Users can tweet out a link to their live stream.

Medium is a blog platform that puts an emphasis on quality content. Users publish their own stories and the community then recommends stories they like.

Blab is a live streaming social network similar to Periscope. It allows the ability to have a live broadcast with up to four people talking in split screen.

Disqus is a social engagement platform. It provides a hosting service for comments posted by users to a blog. It is a great tool for increasing participation and managing feedback on a website.

Viadeo is a professional social network in much the same way as LinkedIn. Founded in France, it has a large number of French users. Having bought social platforms in China, India and a Spanish competitor,[14] its demography is different from LinkedIn.

Vimeo is a video-sharing website. It has an active and engaged community.

Slideshare is primarily a slide-hosting platform, although it also supports documents, PDFs, videos and webinars. It has developed into a great way of sharing presentations with a wider community. It was bought by LinkedIn in 2012.[15]

StumbleUpon creates virtual communities of like-minded web surfers linked by common interests. By rating content, the StumbleUpon web search engine ensures that users 'stumble upon' content of interest recommended by friends and peers.

MySpace – back in 2008, MySpace was the largest social networking site in the world.[16] Although it has been overtaken by many other platforms, it still attracts a significant number of users every month.[17] MySpace was bought by Time Inc. at the beginning of 2016.[18]

This list is by no means exhaustive. Individuals should utilize the platforms most relevant to them, depending on the countries in which they operate and the clientele with whom they need to engage.

As well as these particular platforms, within any industry sector, geographical location and specific audience, salespeople and marketing departments should also consider:

Blogs – these have become huge sources of information and news. Influential bloggers, in any market, can exert a real influence on the community.

Online communities/forums – these are a place where enthusiasts, experts and professionals come together to discuss issues, share knowledge and exchange ideas. There are many very large and dynamic communities around all sorts of sectors and interests.

Media/news sites – there are many platforms dedicated to specific geographical locations, or particular topics, where interested parties interact and engage to keep up with a distinctive passion or concern.

Tools

Once you have decided the relevant platforms on which you will focus your digital selling activities, there are then a number of mechanisms available to facilitate this enterprise.

The tools listed below are by no means exhaustive. The specific platforms are mentioned only as a guide in order to give readers an idea of what is available. In all category types there are other good suppliers that will not have been mentioned. It is up to individuals to choose the most appropriate provider.

It is also worth noting that I have separated out different categories of tools in order to explain the distinct features that are available. However, please note that there is some overlap in the functionality provided by the various offerings.

Social media management and monitoring tools

These tools allow users to monitor conversations taking place online. By using keywords such as their own name, company name and product etc., individuals can listen in when they are being mentioned and choose to respond in an appropriate and timely manner.

The platforms enable people to cut through all the noise, on the different channels, and find the conversations and comments that really matter. Many also provide good data and analytics to enable a greater understanding of the social media landscape and how it pertains to a particular organization.

Examples are:

cyfe.com
hootsuite.com
oktopost.com

sendible.com
socialbakers.com
spredfast.com
sproutsocial.com
sysomos.com
trackur.com
viralheat.com

Customer relationship management (CRM), Social CRM and marketing automation tools

Customer relationship management software has always been important in the sales and marketing process, in order to track customer interactions and use data to spot trends and opportunities.

However, this software traditionally only tracked the interactions between a business and its prospects and customers. Today, of course, there is a great deal of information that customers post about themselves online that would not necessarily have been captured by any personnel in a company. Therefore, social CRM interfaces with social media platforms in order to ensure that businesses have access to this public information about their prospects and customers.

While all this functionality can be found in separate tools, automation features are also often integrated into one platform. This enables a business to track its own interactions with a prospect or customer while being able to see their social media activity. Then, based on their behaviour, automation can be used to assist in nurturing the lead. For example, a sign-up for a webinar may trigger an automated e-mail reminder before the event and offer the prospect an opportunity to download a white paper after it has taken place.

As you can imagine, there are many tools available in this area including:

Adobe Marketing Cloud
batchbook.com
charlieapp.com
hubspot.com
infusionsoft.com

marketo.com
nimble.com
ontraport.com
Oracle Marketing Cloud
pardot.com
salesforce.com
silverpop.com

Website visitor identification software

IP lookup software, combined with relevant databases, allows these platforms to identify many of the anonymous visitors to a website. They will also provide details on what was searched for and the different pages that were viewed.

In the business-to-business arena this can be a very useful tool, as the majority of visitors to a website will not reveal themselves. Knowing who they are allows a business or salesperson to reach out and engage with them in other ways. While many of the CRM and marketing platforms mentioned previously have this functionality built in, other providers include:

a1webstats.com
canddi.com
gatorleads.co.uk
leadfeeder.com
leadforensics.com
visistat.com

Influencer trackers and measurement tools

There are a variety of tools for measuring influence and identifying who the key influencers are in any particular market. Many of these platforms facilitate listening to these influencers and engaging with them. Included in this list are some tools for an individual to measure their own influence:

audiense.com
buzzsumo.com
klout.com

kred.com
socmetrics.com
traackr.com

Keyword finders

Software that provides the ability to identify which are the most appropriate keywords to use can be extremely useful. Some of these platforms work by analysing the competition and providing insights into their advertising, search, linkbuilding and keyword strategies:

authoritylabs.com
compete.com
Google Keyword Planner
longtailpro.com
semrush.com
similarweb.com
spyfu.com

Content curation tools

Curating great content, which means organizing, commenting and sharing it with your own audience, is an effective way of keeping people engaged. There are a number of tools to assist in this endeavour, including:

curata.com
curationsoft.com
curationsuite.com
kudani.com
paper.li
publishthis.com
scoop.it

Content discovery platforms

Ensuring that content is seen by the right audience is vital for being able to earn their attention. Content discovery platforms can assist in making sure material reaches prospects:

content.ad
nativo.net
outbrain.com
revenue.com
taboola.com

Content creation tools

Whether you are trying to create great presentations, animations, infographics, quote image cards, GIFs or memes, there are a large number of tools available to assist, including:

animoto.com
customshow.com
genial.ly
goanimate.com
haikudeck.com
imgur.com
infogr.am
livememe.com
makeagif.com
memedad.com
moovly.com
piktochart.com
powtoon.com
prezi.com
quozio.com
recordit.co
renderforest.com
slideawesome.com
slidebean.com
slidedog.com
slidemagic.com
slides.com
sparkol.com
videoscribe.co

Endnotes

1 Facebook: (2016) Leading social networks worldwide as of January 2016, ranked by number of active users (in millions), *Statista* [online] http://www.statista.com/statistics/272014/global-social-networks-ranked-by-number-of-users/ [accessed 15 March 2016]

'This statistic provides information on the most popular networks worldwide as of January 2016, ranked by number of active accounts. Market leader Facebook was the first social network to surpass 1 billion registered accounts and currently sits at 1.55 billion monthly active users.'

2 Facebook Messenger: (2016) Most popular global mobile messenger apps as of January 2016, based on number of monthly active users (in millions), *Statista*, published January [online] http://www.statista.com/statistics/258749/most-popular-global-mobile-messenger-apps/ [accessed 15 March 2016]

'#1. WhatsApp: 900 #2. Facebook messenger: 800'

3 WhatsApp: Randy Milanovic (2015) The World's 21 Most Important Social Media Sites and Apps in 2015: *Social Media Today*, published 13 April [online] http://www.socialmediatoday.com/social-networks/2015-04-13/worlds-21-most-important-social-media-sites-and-apps-2015 [accessed 15 March 2016]

'The WhatsApp concept is simple: send text-style messages to anyone else using the platform, but without paying data charges. That straightforward idea has already gathered more than 700 million fans, making the app the world's most popular messaging platform.'

4 Facebook/WhatsApp: Parmy Olson (2014) Facebook closes $19 billion WhatsApp deal: *Forbes/Tech*, published 6 October [online] http://www.forbes.com/sites/parmyolson/2014/10/06/facebook-closes-19-billion-whatsapp-deal/#5c4465ba179e [accessed 15 March 2016]

'The acquisition has gone through a few regulatory hoops, but it passed the final one last Friday when the European Union gave it the green light.'

5 Instagram: (2016) Top 15 most popular photo sharing sites | May 2016, *eBizMBA*, published 1 March [online] http://www.ebizmba.com/articles/photo-sharing-sites [accessed 15 May 2016]

'#1 | *Instagram 72 – eBizMBA Rank | 100,000,000 – Estimated Unique Monthly Visitors | 50 – Compete Rank | 128 – Quantcast Rank | 37 – Alexa Rank | Last Updated: March 1, 2016. The Most Popular Photo Sharing Sites | eBizMBA.*'

Author notes: eBizMBA updates its rankings monthly – the above statistics are correct as of May 2016.

6   Facebook/Instagram: (2012) Facebook buys Instagram photo sharing network for $1bn: *BBC*, published 10 April [online] http://www.bbc.co.uk/news/technology-17658264 [accessed 15 March 2016]

'Facebook has announced it is to buy Instagram – the popular photo-sharing smartphone app. Facebook is paying $1bn (£629m) in cash and stock for the takeover.'

7   Narrative reference: Randy Milanovic (2015) The world's 21 most important social media sites and apps in 2015, *Social Media Today*, published 13 April [online] http://www.socialmediatoday.com/social-networks/2015-04-13/worlds-21-most-important-social-media-sites-and-apps-2015#sthash.9LWPPiHV.dpuf [accessed 15 March 2016]

'18. vk.com. Promoting itself as Europe's largest social media site, vk.com is essentially the Russian version of Facebook, with the same kinds of profiles, messaging, and games you would expect.'

8   Google: (2016) Desktop search engine market share, *NetMarketShare.com*, published February [online] https://www.netmarketshare.com/search-engine-market-share.aspx?qprid=4&qpcustomd=0 [accessed 15 March 2016]

'Google (Global) – 71.35%, Bing – 12.37%, Baidu – 7.34%, Yahoo (Global) – 7.20%' (plus four others)

Author notes: eBizMBA updates its rankings monthly – the above statistics are correct as of April 2016.

9   Twitter/Vine: Drew Olanoff (2013) Just six months after being acquired, Twitter's Vine hits #1 free spot on Apple's App Store, *TechCrunch.com*, published 8 April [online] http://techcrunch.com/2013/04/08/just-six-months-after-being-acquired-twitters-vine-hits-1-free-spot-on-apples-app-store/ [accessed 15 March 2016]

'Twitter acquired the mini-video-taking app Vine last October before it ever launched, sending everyone into a frenzy about the company getting into the video space.'

10 Narrative reference (2016) Top 15 most popular video websites | May 2016: *EbizMBA*, published 14 May [online] http://www.ebizmba.com/ articles/video-websites [accessed 15 March 2016]

'# 1 | YouTube 3 - eBizMBA Rank | 1,000,000,000 - Estimated Unique Monthly Visitors | 4 - Compete Rank | 2 - Quantcast Rank | 3 - Alexa Rank | Last Updated: May 14 2016. The Most Popular Video Websites | eBizMBA.'

Author notes: eBizMBA updates its rankings monthly – the above statistics are correct as of May 2016.

11 YouTube #2: Elise Moreau (2016) The top 25 social networking sites people are using, *About.com*, published 13 February [online] http:// webtrends.about.com/od/socialnetworkingreviews/tp/Social-Networking-Sites.htm [accessed 15 March 2016]

'After Google, YouTube is the second largest search engine.'

12 Google/YouTube: Michael Arrington (2006) Google has acquired YouTube, *TechCrunch*, published 9 October [online] http://techcrunch. com/2006/10/09/google-has-acquired-youtube/ [accessed 15 March 2016]

'Moments ago the deal was confirmed. In their largest acquisition to date, Google has acquired YouTube for $1.65 billion in an all stock transaction.'

13 Twitter/Periscope: Yoree Koh and Evelyn M Rusli (2015) Twitter acquires live-video streaming startup Periscope, *Wall Street Journal*, published 9 March [online] http://www.wsj.com/articles/twitter-acquires-live-video-streaming-startup-periscope-1425938498 [accessed 15 March 2016]

'Twitter Inc. has quietly purchased Periscope, which had been developing a live-video streaming app...'

14 Viadeo: (Undated) Company information, *Wikipedia* [online] https:// en.wikipedia.org/wiki/Viadeo [accessed 15 March 2016]

'From November 2006 to August 2007, Viadeo raised... funding from investors. Later that year, Viadeo announced the acquisition of Tianji.com, a Chinese business social network... in July 2008 Viadeo acquired its Spanish competitor ICTnet... In early 2009, Viadeo

acquired the Indian professional social networks services, ApnaCircle.'

15 LinkedIn/Slideshare: Eric Savitz (2012) LinkedIn to buy SlideShare for $118.75M; Q1 crushes estimates, *Forbes*, published 3 May [online] http://www.forbes.com/sites/ericsavitz/2012/05/03/linkedin-to-buy-slideshare-for-118-75m-q1-crushes-estimates/#3dd556a870f9 [accessed 15 March 2016]

'LinkedIn this afternoon announced a deal to buy the professional content-sharing site SlideShare for $118.75 million in cash and stock.'

16 MySpace 2008: Craig Smith (2015) By the numbers: 17 MySpace stats and facts then and now, *DMR*, published 14 August [online] http://expandedramblings.com/index.php/myspace-stats-then-now/ [accessed 15 March 2016]

'Number of MySpace users at its peak: 75.9 million. Month/Year of MySpace's peak: December 2008.'

17 MySpace users: Mike Shields (2015) MySpace still reaches 50 million people each month, *Wall Street Journal*, published 14 January [online] http://blogs.wsj.com/cmo/2015/01/14/myspace-still-reaches-50-million-people-each-month/ [accessed 15 March 2016]

'Did you know that 50 million people still visit MySpace each month? Would you be surprised that MySpace users generated over 300 million video views in November, good enough for 16th place on comScore's Video Metrix ranking?'

18 Narrative reference: Jasper Jackson (2016) Time Inc buys what is left of MySpace for its user data, *Guardian*, published 11 February [online] http://www.theguardian.com/media/2016/feb/11/time-inc-buys-what-is-left-of-myspace-for-its-user-data [accessed 15 March 2016]

'Time Inc has acquired what is left of social media pioneer MySpace in a move designed to hoover up user data to help it target digital ads more effectively.'

although salespeople gave out the brochures and literature produced by marketing, many would articulate that these materials provided minimal assistance in winning business. Today, however, salespeople require more considerable support from marketing departments.

For example, it is not realistic for salespeople to produce the content they require to support their online channels on their own. Therefore, there needs to be a closer relationship with marketing, who should be able to assist in some of the creation, curation and commissioning of material. Moreover, it might be marketing that uses software to identify influencers in a particular sector. It may then be left to salespeople to approach the influencers in order to build relationships and explore ways of working together.

Today, marketing teams will be utilizing digital media in a variety of ways. From websites to blogs, from social media channels to forums, marketing personnel will be involved in a multitude of activities. However, in many ways, salespeople have become micro marketers. They will also be using social media channels that require content in order to establish credibility, attract new opportunities and raise their profile amongst target communities. One can quickly ascertain that without close cooperation, this situation could become a real mess.

Of course, how sales and marketing teams structure themselves will depend on the organization for which they work and the sectors and environments in which they operate. While it is unhelpful to be too prescriptive, there are lines of delineation which can be used as a guide in order for sales and marketing teams to work together effectively.

There are some business-to-consumer brands that generate excitement and passion, and people are willing to interact and follow them on social media channels. However, this is unusual. For many organizations, and certainly in the business-to-business world, social media is not a brand-to-person communication tool. People do not want to interact or have conversations with a faceless company, but with other individuals. Obviously, there are platforms such as websites, company blogs and company social media pages that come under the brand remit, but in order to be engaging, many of the interactions online will necessarily be person to person. Essentially, marketing should be responsible for the brand and company communications, while salespeople should take control of the person-to-person conversations.

In this way, we can start to see how sales and marketing can support each other and work extremely effectively together while having a clear delineation of responsibilities. The analogy I would use is to think of marketing as the directors and producers of the film, with the sales team as the actors. Of course, in order for this to be possible, there has to be strategic alignment between sales and marketing. The teams should sit in the same department and have regular meetings and communications so both have sight of the other's activities.

The top line strategy, that is, defining the ethos of the business, the value proposition and emotional selling proposition, as explained in Chapter 3, should be owned by the marketing department. However, these decisions should necessarily be taken at board level, as they are of such vital strategic importance to the business as a whole. Therefore, the sales director and marketing director should both be part of establishing this vision along with the other senior 'C-Suite' executives.

It is essential to note, at this juncture, that the senior executives of any organization should have a social media presence. While this will fall under the remit of marketing, as the directors and producers, it is vital that an enterprise purporting to be using social channels seriously has its senior team utilizing these platforms. Without this leadership there is less likely to be enthusiasm within the business. Moreover, the outside world will conclude that the company does not hold these channels in high regard if the senior management of the organization has no presence on any of these networks.

With marketing owning the strategy, it is they who should be conducting ongoing research into the state of the market and following the influencers in order to be able to feed insights to the sales team, as well as the wider organization. Meanwhile, salespeople should be charged with feeding back the market intelligence they glean from the interactions they have with prospects and clients.

With this constant focus on the changing market, keeping up with the influencers, and collating all sorts of customer intelligence, it is ultimately the marketing team that is responsible for creating, curating and commissioning content. Some of this material will necessarily be used for corporate communications on the website, company blog and social media pages. However, marketing should be liaising with sales in order to produce content that can be used by different individual sales staff with a focus on their own markets and sectors etc.

While in collaboration with marketing, salespeople can obviously create their own content, but marketing should also enable and facilitate some of this production. For example, marketing may organize a video shoot giving salespeople the chance to be interviewed about their particular sector. In this way, they can provide value for their prospects and clientele and have material that can be used on their own blog or social media pages.

With the delineation between sales and marketing established, and constant collaboration taking place, it becomes easier to separate different activities. For example, it will be the marketing team who will be responsible for following influencers and identifying strategic partners, although sales personnel will obviously be able to offer ideas at various times. However, it will fall to salespeople to establish these relationships and find ways of working together in order to leverage each other's audience and create new value for prospects and customers. It will also be salespeople who are tasked with obtaining testimonials on public platforms from existing customers.

Where there are overlaps between the roles, these can still be clearly defined. So, for example, the salesperson's Digital Sales Funnel will be their part of a much bigger entity, which marketing must be able to monitor and measure. However, by having a specific tag within the CRM system, it will be relatively straightforward for an individual salesperson to be able to measure and understand their own Digital Sales Funnel from the wider company.

Similarly, while marketing will operate the social media monitoring software, an individual salesperson will have an account with their own name and, for example, the specific products with which they work as keywords. In this way, salespeople can respond and stay on top of the prospects, customers and others that comment on their sectors or areas of expertise. Meanwhile, marketing will respond to the more generic company remarks or tag them for the relevant salesperson.

In the same way, the company website will be owned by the marketing department. However, working closely with the sales department will enable individual salespeople to request that specific landing pages are created, and that the leads are passed on to the appropriate individuals within an organization.

While I make no attempt to be prescriptive, or to suggest that one solution is entirely suitable for every organization, there is a blueprint for how sales and marketing teams can work together. In the digital environment this is essential. The final consideration is to ensure that targets and incentives are aligned between the sales and marketing departments, so that both will be aiming for the same goals instead of trying to pursue diametrically opposed targets, which does sometimes occur within companies.

We are living through an era of profound change. The ubiquity of the internet, world wide web and digital technology has totally changed many of the paradigms by which commercial enterprises operated for many years.

Digital selling provides readers with an insight into the strategies, platforms and tools necessary to thrive in today's business environment. By utilizing the Digital Sales Funnel and understanding the way it can be measured effectively, organizations are able to ensure they can assess the productivity of their sales and marketing functions and look to constantly improve. With the understanding digital selling provides, companies can comprehend how to utilize the digital channels available in the most potent way. The threats are real but the opportunities are immense.

So, ensure you and your organization avoid suffering from Pike Syndrome, and embrace the world of digital selling.

INDEX

Note: *Italics* indicate a Figure or Table in the text.